Rice Economy and Kerala Model of Clustering

Rice Economy and Kerala Model of Clustering

K. Krishnadas

SERIALS PUBLICATIONS
NEW DELHI (INDIA)

First Published - 2009

ISBN: 978-81-8387-277-5

Published by

SERIALS PUBLICATIONS
4830/24, Prahlad Street, Ansari Road
Darya Ganj, New Delhi-110002 (India)
Phone : 23245225 Fax : 91-11-23272135
E-mail: serials@satyam.net.in

Dedicated to

My Beloved Father

The Late

K. R. Kesava Panicker

Contents

FOREWORD

The book *"Rice economy and Kerala Model of Clustering"* deals in depth the various contributing factors of rice mill clustering in Kalady. The study is carried out interpreting the concept of economic geography and economics of clustering from the point of view of location theory in a vivid and threadbare manner. The study amply supports the cluster concept i.e. what industrial activities are located where and why? The concept of external economics plays a crucial role in rice mill clustering in Kalady. The book makes an analytical and critical appraisal regarding various "push" factors of rice mill clustering at Kalady. The distance to market, demand for product, availability of raw materials, nearness to River Periyar and lot of other factors play a significant role in the spatial aspects of concentration of modern rice mills in and around Kalady. The concentration of modern rice mills in Kalady offers a pooled market for workers with industry specific skills, ensuring a lower probability of unemployment and a higher probability of profit. The spill-over benefit of rice clustering offers a better and congenial production environment of rice mill owners. All these properties are logically and methodically well knit in the present book.

The deceleration trend in paddy cultivation in Kerala and Ernakulam district is an alarming factor. The main reason for deceleration can be attributed to the negative impact of cropping pattern in Kerala. The financial aspect of modern rice mills under study clearly portraits a picture of effective and proper utilization of capital and long term funds in both fixed and working capital. The author high lights the agricultural and related scenario of Kerala with craft and in genuity of an agricultural scientist. The deceleration of rice production poses a great threat to food security and is likely to be a backward pulling force (pull factor), to the modern rice mill clustering in future. This is a force that tends to oppose geographical concentration. It took decades and decades for a fine tuned transformation of rice processing from a house hold business to modern techno-savvy clustering in Kalady. In spite of thick geographical concentration of paddy fields in Plakkad and Alappuzha districts of Kerala, Kalady was able to emerge as a successful industrial rice location due to generation of linkages associated with rice production along with strong historical reasons. Kalady has become an amazing trading centre of rice and rice products, thus earning an indelible status in the industrial map of Kerala. This adds an additional feather in the cap of Kalady, other wise well known as the birth place of Adi Sankara, one of the world famous philosophers.

To put it in a nutshell the book will be a scholarly asset to any one who carefully peruse it, a feast to others who glance through the chapters, a beautiful and crisp guide to entrepreneur, a thematic work for researchers, and a schematic financial performance analysis for readers with commerce background.

The findings of the book will be a stimulus to policy makers, administrators and academicians to the revival of the multi farius aspects relating to clustering, rice production, paddy cultivation and cropping pattern. The analytical rigor, plausible observations and intelligent deductions are worth mentioning. The book stands unique in all aspects. My profound tributes to Dr. K. Krishnadas and to his enduring efforts to bring forth this illustrious work.

Kalady,
20-01-2009

Dr. P. S. Mohanakumar
Reader and Head,
P.G.Department of Economics and
Research Centre,
Sree Sankara College, Kalady,

PREFACE

The present study *"Rice Economy and Kerala Model of Clustering"*, analyses the causes and factors that led to the clustering of rice mills in and around Kalady. Applicability of Porter's Diamond model of clustering along with the financial performance and problems. The study is mainly based on both primary and secondary data for the period 2000 to 2005. Out of the 120 modern rice mills in the state 80 are located in Ernakulam District with a cluster of 52 modern rice mills in and around Kalady. Out of this 42 modern rice mills are selected as sample units to analyse the reasons and effects of conglomeration of rice mills, 20 mills are selected for financial performance analysis. The trend in output growth is decomposed in to the yield effect, area effect and cropping pattern effect to analyse the deceleration of rice production in Kerala based on secondary data for a period of 30 years from 1974-75 to 2003-04. The study result shows that the factors that led to the clustering of rice mills in Kalady are location specific viz entrepreneurial growth and availability of pure water form perennial water source of river Periyar. The financial result shows that all the 20 modern rice mills are running at a profit and technically advanced mills (Fully - Automated) are having an edge over sales than the less advanced mills (semi-automated). The long term borrowings and capital are effectively invested in fixed assets and working capital in the rice mills under study. The real cause for the deceleration of rice production in the state of Kerala is identified as negative change in the cropping pattern effect which also created a serious problem of raw material shortage. The other problems identified as cost of electricity, transport cost, high input cost, un healthy competition, poor linkage with supporting industries etc.

ABBREVIATIONS

IRRI	:	International Rice ResearchInstitute
CRRI	:	Central Rice Research Institute.
CMIE	:	Centre for Monitoring Indian Economy.
CBRI	:	Central Board Research Institute.
R&D	:	Research & Development.
RRI	:	Regional Research institute
UNDP	:	United Nations Development Programme.
GOVT	:	Government
Ha	:	Hectare
DIST	:	District
AOA	:	Agreement on Agriculture
KRMC	:	KaladyRice Millers Consortium
KRMOA	:	Kerala Rice Mill Owners Association
CSIR	:	Council of Scientific Research
ICAR	:	Indian Council for Agricultural Research
WHO	:	World Health Organization
CFTRI	:	Central Food Technology Research Institute
IIT	:	Indian Institute of Technology
RPEC	:	Rice Processing Engineering Centre, IIT, Kharagpur
MT	:	Metric Tonne.
LT	:	Lakh Tonne.
GP	:	Gross Profit.
NP	:	Net Profit.
BS	:	Balance Sheet.

BC	:	Before Christ.
AD	:	After Death (Anna Domini).
HYV	:	High Yielding Variety.
GOK	:	Govern ment of Kerala.
LT	:	Lower Transmission.
A/C	:	Account.
CPCRI	:	Central Plantations Crops Research institute.
FAO	:	Food and Agricultural Organization.
GOI	:	Government of India.
DCSSI	:	Development Commissioner Small Scale Industries.
MML	:	Margin Money Loan.
CFCE	:	Common Facility Centre Expeller.
SEA	:	Solvent Extractors Association (of India).
K F C	:	Kerala Financial Corporation.
SIDBI	:	State Industries Development Bank of India.

1

Introduction

Agriculture is the oldest and most important avocation of the world. The human society is dependent upon agriculture for its food, clothing and shelter. At certain stages of human development it used to be the only known means of living. Even today in the highly developed industrial countries, agriculture plays a major role as the supplier of rawmaterials for industries and commerce apart from its basic role in supplying food, clothing and shelter. Therefore the welfare of a state to a large extent is dependent upon the prosperity of its agriculture.

Agriculture is the major sector of economic activity. It provides not only food and raw materials but also employment to a very large proportion of population. Agriculture is the source of livelihood for more than two third of our population. It remains the back bone of our economy.

Agriculture is the corner stone of development. Indian agriculture is known for its multi-functions of providing employment, lively hood, food, nutritional and ecological securities.

In a country like India, where more than 80 per cent of the population living in rural areas and more than two third of our population dependent on agriculture and allied sector, the need for rural base industries–especially agro based should be more emphasized. Agrobased industries in our countryside hold great promise to bring about substantial improvement in the quality of life of rural people. With continuous increase in labour force in rural areas and declining employment opportunities in agriculture, these industries will play an increasingly important role in income and employment generation in the coming decades. There should, therefore be a proper integration and coordination between agriculture and industry to ensure intensive and extensive development of agriculture, there by creating additional employment for the rural population.

The growth of agro based industries help in raising the standard of living of the rural population by providing them more income, consumer goods at cheeper rates and social economic overheads. An expanding agriculture sector increase the demand for non-farm inputs like fertilizers, agricultural machinery, and implements manufactured in the non-agricultural sector. The stimulus received by the industrial sector in turn increases the demand for wage, goods and rawmaterials which help to expand agriculture employment and income.

This is in turn creates market demand for consumer goods of industrial origin by providing a future stimulus to industrialization and development of market. The tertioary sector also expand with the development of trade and commerce. In addition to production of food articles agriculture is the main supplier of rawmaterials to industries. The significance of this role depends on the importance of agro based industries in the total industrial sector. It may be recalled that industrialization in India started with the setting up of factories for processing of agriculture commodities or manufacturing industries whose rawmateri als were produced on farms. There has been significant diversification of agriculture and the agrobased industries in number and expanded their production during the last few decades.

Agriculture transformation through creation of forward and backward linkages with industry is a recently emerged phenomenon. Our farmers efforts in using Green Revolution technologies are strengthing our food and income security. While a part of the surplus production is stored in our buffer stocks, the remaining portion is yet to attract the value addition chain-the key for agricultural growth.

The term agro based industries implies proximity and affinity between agriculture and industry. Generally agrobased industries may be divided into two groups - input based and output based. Input based industries may be defined as those industries whose products serve as inputs to the agricultural sector.

Agro Based Industries are Industries which:

1. Lead to better processing and conversion of agricultural commodities.
2. Increase agriculture production.
3. Ensure high returns to the value added products.

Agro Based Industries can be Divided into two Categories:

1. Capital Intensive Processing Industries and
2. Labour Intensive Processing Industries

In the case of Capital Intensive Processing Industries the capital involved will be larger. Hence the persons employed will require some amount of technical training of knowledge. The processing industries that use agriculture products as its raw-materials are Rice Processing Mills, Sugar Industries, Oil seed industries, cotton industries, Tobacco industries, Fruits and Vegetable processing units. Among agro-industries, rice processing industry is the biggest industry in India because India is the largest producer of rice next only to China.

Among agro-industries, rice processing industry is the biggest industry in India. Rice is one of the important agricultural commodities in the world. It is obtained by processing paddy. More than 50 per cent of the worlds population consumes rice as their main food. But it is significant to note that world trade in rice is less than five per cent of the total production. In India food grain production has increased almost four times since independence. In Kerala, rice is the staple food. Rice processing industry is one of the traditional industries in Kerala. The present study enquires about the growth and development of rice trading. It is to be noted that the growth and development of rice trading will lead to solve the problems of unemployment to a greater extend. The present study is proposed to chart out the role that can be played by rice mills in Kerala. The study also analyses different aspects such as declining of economic activity due to paddy field conversion, change in cropping pattern that resulted declining of area as well as production of rice. In Kerala, the production of rice is deteriorating every year, this creates widening the supply gap in food grains. The decline of rice production created irreverssible threat on Kerala's food security. The importance of rice processing get enhanced because of the following factors.

These processing units can very well effectively utilize the raw material of local cultivation.

These industries facilitate to change the traditional method of processing to sophisticated technology by establishing rice mills in the modern lines.

These industries will help the growth of entrepreneurship in rural areas and it will help to generate employment and provide job for rural workers.

These industries can make the village life more livable by providing basic amenities.

These industries in the rural level can very well absorb surplus labour force which is a common phenomenon with agriculture employment.

These industries can very well avoid the exploitation of middle men in the rice trade as they can directly purchase raw material from the farmers in the village level.

The modernization of rice mill are capital intensive the government can provide more fund to the village enterprises to convert their traditional mills to modern lines.

As these industries are started on modern lines they can export their products to foreign countries and can earn foreign exchange.

These industries can foster self confidence and to encourage qualities of leadership, initiative and enterprise among the rural youth.

Paddy processing industry is one of the traditional industries in Kerala. Earlier paddy processing was considered as a house hold business. As time passed, with the increase in production and productivity of paddy, rice mills on modern lines began to flourish. Paddy production is highly concentrated in the districts of Palakkad and Alappuzha Districts in Kerala. These two areas are known as the 'rice bowls' of Kerala. The increase in output of paddy in these two districts, there happened progressive growth in the establishment of rice mills in Ernakulam District. It is highly significant to note that out of 120 modern Rice Mills in Kerala, 80 are located in Ernakulam Dist. This is about 67 per cent of the total modern rice mills in the state. Out of this 80 modern rice mills in Ernakulam District 52 modern rice mills are located in and around Kalady. This resulted a cluster development of rice mills in Kalady.

The growth pattern of the rice mills in Kerala and its conglomeration in and around Kalady in Ernakulam District can be essentially viewed from the angle of some well established and accepted logical theoretical derivations. The staunch champion and father of Economics - Adam Smith - in his earlier writings put a strong plea for the development of the specialization and division of labour so as to increase production. Though this can be interpreted as a statement which is having a generality, when one peep into prose and corns of the statement one can understand that it has its own relevance in the expansion of individual sectors. Hence the views of Smith can be followed from the point of view of the reason for specialization and conglomeration . David Ricardo, one of the veterans in the classical trio-launched his Comparitive Advantage Theory which essentially stated the production and transfer of items in which a country posses comparitive advantage. When this view is transplanted into the spectrum of the industrial clusterings viz rice mill cluster one can very well substantiate that the very existence of this clusters can be some how or other related to the comparative advantages emerged from clustering. The neo classical stalwart Alfred Marshall demonstrated the essential nature of the then prevailed small and tiny industrial units and their relative growth by absorbing its comparitive advantage which essentially resulted from conglomeration of these units. He pin-pointed the basic fact that of higher efficiency meeted out by these firms. This view may be practically labelled as a forerunner of modern theories on clustering, so the essential nature of functioning of rice mill industry possibly linked towards this theoretical view point.

Modern theoretical development relating to the clustering aspects of industries are primarily due to the work of Porter (1998). Porter had improved upon the earlier writings of Smith and Ricardo and devised a special theoretical logic especially labelled as Diamond Theory. Porter shifted the scheme of analysis to specific industries and pinpointed the benefits derived from product differentiation, competitiveness, technological development, economics of scale and the relative size of the market.

The crucial factors which shaped the diamond theory are (1) The firm strategy, (2) structure and rivalry (3) Conditions of factor supply (4) The structure of demand conditions (5) Supporting Industries (6) Competition that can be emerged within the industry.

In addition to these major aspects government policy and chance variables influence the above determinants. So the above six factors altogether influence the proper shaping of the structure of the conglomeration. These aspects exert its relative influence upon the conglomeration depending upon the size and structure of the conglomeration.

The diamond theory outlined above encompasses the following special features.

1. The inter related group of firms and institutions in a particular field of particular area.
2. Value creation and addition
3. Firm strategy structure and rivalry factor conditions and demand conditions of related and supporting industries.

Basing Porters diamond theory a novel attempt is done, so as to elicitate the nature and process of the factors governing and influencing the conglomeration of rice mills in Ernakulam District in and around Kalady–the granary of rice mills.

Paddy is a main crop in Kerala. Kerala has succeeded in developing a very good rice processing and packaging infrastructure to bring about stew of rice brands in to the market. But the production of rice deteriorated from year to year in Kerala. The rice mills in the state are concentrated mainly in and around Kalady. The study aims to analyse the factors that lead to the clustering of rice mills in and around Kalady. The present study also proposes to analyse the financial performance of rice mills in and around Kalady.

Since rice is a major crop of Kerala and the majority of farmers in the state are rice farmers, the prosperity of the people of Kerala is based on the performance of the rice crop and hence Kerala's economy is largely rice based. The study also aims to go through the decline in paddy cultivation in Kerala. The declining trend in paddy cultivation has resulted a significant lowering of total rice production in the state thuswidening the self sufficiency, of predominantly rice eating population of Kerala. The present annual production is nearly 1/6 of the estimated requirement of rice in Kerala. The reasons for the wide gap between the demand and the actual production also need special attention from policy makers.

CONCEPTUAL FRAME WORK

To have an unambiguous theoretical explanations and logical conclusions the present study utilized some terms and concepts. The utilization of concepts and terms in this study are essentially related to the actual theoretical derivations, but some conceptualisation are made in the usage so as to have a better clarity to the explanation of facts. For the attainment of the general and specific objectives out lined in the study the following terms and concepts are used.

CLUSTERING

A cluster can be defined as a group of firms engaged in a particular product market in a particular location.

"A Cluster can be deifned as a gorup of firm sengaged in a particular product market in a particular location." (Porter 1998). "A Group of producers making similar thigns in close vicinity to each other". (Sebumitz 1995).

"Cluster is an industrial district, ie a core of more-or-less equal small enterprises bound in a complex web of competition and co-operation. (Piore and Sabel 1984).

Rice Mill

Paddy and Milling was a traditional business in Kerala. Decades back each family was having its own paddy for their requirements and boil it and mill traditionally. Slowly the system changed and people preferred to purchase rice due to convenience and milling is done by most sophisticated rice mills known as modern rice mills.

Conglomeration

This is the physical presence of a system of activity concentrating in a particular space having more or less homogeneous features, acting with a mission of physical out put orientation.

Agro Based Industry

Agro Based Industries which depend on agriculture for the supply of raw materials. This is effect of forward linkage.

Agro-processing Industry

Processing of farm products to consumer commodities and in the process reduces wastage, increases shelf-life which resulting in value addition and higher income transfer to the farmers. The most prominent activity in food grains processing is primarily milling of paddy.

FINANCIAL PERFORMANCE

Profitability is best regarded as earnings generated in relation to the resources invested in a firms activities.

In the theory of the firm, and also in business practice, the eocnomics of a firm can be looked from two points of view, the static and the dynamic. In the theory of the firm the static aspect is reflected in the value of the firm, and the dynamic aspect is reflected in the charges of this vlaue during a peirod. In business practice, the fianncial performance means the financial standing and dynamic aspect means the annual performance. The balance sheet reflect the financial standing and the income statement for evaluating the performance of the firm.

CAPACITY

The ability of an industry to produce with present resources and facilities which it commands is called the capacity of an industry. The capacity levels are maximum or theoretical capacity, practical or operating capacity, actual capacity, idle capacity etc.

Marketing Strategy

It is the strategy adopted either by a producer or a distributor to supply goods and services to the ultimate users by way of different channels of distribution.

Ratio Analysis

Meaning of Ratio: A ratio is a mathematical relationship between two related items expressed in quantitative form. When this definition of ratio is explained with reference to the items shown in financial statements, it is called 'accounting ratio'. An accounting ratio is defined as quantitative relationship between two or more items of the financial statements connected with each other. This quantitative relationship may be expressed in the following ways.

(a) In proportion. In this form the amounts of the two items are being expressed in a Common denominator. For eg. The relationship between current assets and current liabilities as 2:1.

(b) In Ratio or Times or Co-efficient: In this form, a quotient obtained by dividing one items by another items is taken as unit of expression. The example of this form is sales divided by stock. When ratio is expressed in this form it is called as "turnover" and is written in times.

(c) In percentage: In this form, a quotient obtained by dividing one item by another is multiplied by one hundred and it becomes the 'percentage' form of expression. The relation between gross profit and sales may be expressed as 25%.

SIGNIFICANCE OF RATIO ANALYSIS

(i) The business facts shown in financial statements, do not carry any importance individually. Their importance lies in the fact that they are inter-related. Hence there is need for establishing relationship between various but related items, if any correct and accurate conclusion is to be drawn by their use.

(ii) *Ratio:* Ratio analysis as a tool for the interpretation of financial statements is also significant because ratios help the analyst to have a deep peep into the data given in statements. Figure in their absolute forms shown in financial statements are neither significant nor able to be compared.

SOCIAL RELEVANCE OF THE STUDY

Rice is the staple food of Kerala. It is the major crop of Kerala and majority of farmers in the state are rice farmers. The prosperity of the people of Kerala is rice based on the performance of the rice crop and hence Kerala's economy is rice based. The area and production of rice which was steadily increasing till mid seventies succumb to economic pressure emanating from other remunerative crops like coconut, rubber, banana etc.There is a decline of more than 5 lakh hectors of area under paddy cultivation during the last two decades. This increased the gap between the demand and supply of the main food of Kerala.Now the production of rice is less than 15% of the total requirement of food grains. The other valuable services provided by the paddy fields should also be considered.

In order to increase the production and cultivation of rice in the state, it is necessary to bring a legislation protecting paddy fields in lines with the Conservation and Protection of Forest

Act passed by the Central Govern ment and it should be included in the IXth Schedule of the Constitution of India, other wise with in a short span of time the remaining paddy fields will also dis appear causing serious food shortage in the years to come.

Since agriculture is the major source of economic activity in the world, the human society is depending upon agriculture for its basic requirements. Apart from this it also supplies raw material to the agro based industries. In India alone more than 80 per cent of the population depend on agriculture and allied activities. Among the agro based industries- food processing industry is the largest in terms of production, consumption, export and growth prospective. More over the huge population base of 1.08 billion, growing at an average of 1.6 per cent per annum provides large and growing domestic market for the food products. Rice and rice products have the very bright scope for value addition and value creation.

In Kerala, rice processing industries have very bright future for expansion. Rice processing industries in the state of Kerala has enormous significance as there is wide gap between the demand and supply of rice–the staple food of Kerala. This bring a great social relevance to the present study.

RESEARCH DESIGN

Research Issues : The basic research issues/questions of this study are enlisted below:

1. What are the real causes for the deceleration of rice production in Kerala?
2. What are the locational factors that influence the congloreration of rice mill in around Kalady.
3. To what extent the rice mills in an around Kalady satisfies Porter's diamond model of clustering?
4. What is the financial performance of this agro processing units–rice mills in Kalady?

GENERAL OBJECTIVES

The overall objectives of the present study is to provide a thorough enquiry into the growth and progress of rice mill business in and around Kalady. The study also aims to analyse the specific problems faced by the rice mill buisness in Kerala generally and rice mill units in Kalady specifically. In more precise terms, the following are the specific objectives of the present investigaiton.

The specific objectives of the study are:

1. To evaluate the deceleration in rice produciton due the negative impact of the cropping pattern in Kerala.
2. To enquire in to the factors contributed to the conglomoration of modern rice mill in and around Kalady ie. to isolate the locaitonal cmponents in the growth of modern rice mills in Kalady.
3. To address the case of rice milling cluster in terms of Porters Diamond Model of clustering.
4. To evaluate the financial performance of modern rice mill business in and around Kalady.

HYPOTHESES

1. The deceleration in produciton of rice is due to negative change in cropping pattern effect in the state of Kerala.
2. There is a positive relation between entrepreneurial growth and availability of pure water resulted in the clusteirng of rice mills in Kalady.
3. Technical progress bears a positive influence on sales.
4. Technically progressed mills have lesser debt-equity ratio.
5. The capital and long term borrowing are effectively invested in fixed assets and working capital (Current Assets) of the rice mill business.

METHODOLOGY

The study is an empirical one, based mainly on primary data. The data required for the study are collected from both published and unpublished data. Primary data is used for collecting primary level information. In addition to this surveys, interviews and discussions among the workers and traders of rice, and the owners of rice mills are also done. Secondary data were obtained from the published sources.

Details regarding production, Marketing financial position etc. were collected from the Audited Accounts and Balance Sheets for a period of five years (2000-01 to 2004-05).

The study also makes an analysis of the deceleration of rice produciton in Kerala, its impact on the main foodprocessing industry of Kerala ie. rice processing mills. The present study on declaining of rice production of Kerala pertains to the peirod form 1974-75 to 2003-04. The data on area, production and yield of rice are collected form the vairous publicaitons of the Govenrment of Kerala.

Selection of Respondents

For the purpose of conducting the present study the following methodological device is employed for sample section. Out of a total of 120 Modern Rice mills in the state of Kerala 80 of them are located in Ernakulam district. Out of 80 rice mills located in Ernakulam district 52 are in Kalady and surrounding areas. The total number of rice mills in the research site are listed. This denotes the total number (universe) of the units. In the case of rice mills in Ernakulam district numbered 80 units are considered. Giving proportional weight to each strata, the sample number 42 were taken for the study. (35% in the state, 52.5% in Ernakulam District).

20 modern rice mills are selected as samples for analysing financial performance on the basis of market surveys based on printed questionaires. These rice mills together contribute 30 per cent of the total market share of branded rice. The number of modern rice mills selected for financial performance analysis is 20 which is equal to 17% in the state and 25% in Ermakulam District.

Techniques Applied

Statistical tools like trend analysis, linear regression, annual average growth rates, Correlation proportion test, Z test etc. have been applied for arriving at the conclusions. In addition to the above mentioned statistical tools, Management accounting tools like Ratio analysis and Cash flow Analysis etc are used for anlaysing the data. Simple mathematical tools like percentages, averages, trend projection method are also used for the analysis of the data.

Data Sources

The materials for the study have been collected from various sources namely primary and secondary.

Primary Data

The primary data for the study are collected from merchants associations, Kalady Rice Millers Consortium (KRMC) Rice mill owners Associations, field survey among rice mill owners etc. Employees and Trade Union leaders related to the rice mills were also interviewed.

Secondary Data

The secondary data used for the study are collected from the following sources.

1. Annual Economic Reviews published by the State Planning Board, Government of Kerala.
2. Data Book on Agriculture Published by the State Planning Board, Government of Kerala.
3. Annual Audited Accounts of Rice mills selected as sample units.
4. Annual survey of Industries–Directorate of Economics and Statistics, Government of Kerala.
5. Statistical statements relating to the production, area of cultivation etc. from various Krishi Bhavans in the State and other publishing agencies and individual researchers.
6. Various Journals, Articles, Reports Published by Central Government.
7. Land Resources of Kerala State, published by Kerala State, Land use Board, Thiruvananthapuram.
8. Various Books, Journals, Reports etc. published by Kerala Agricultural University.
9. Various Books, Journals, Reports etc. published by central plantation crops Research Institute.

10. Book, Journals, Reports, relating to the Topic of research.

REVIEW OF THE EARLIER STUDIES

Several studies were conducted with regard to the agro-processing mainly the Rice Mill Industries in Kerala. But some how or other these studies were essentially concentrated on the aspects like the processing of paddy, the impact of mechanaisation, and the employee–employer relationship in this sector.

So far no comprehensive study is known to have conducted by giving special emphasis to the evaluation of the production, marketing, financial aspects, clustering and capacity utilization aspects of Rice Mill Industries.

According to Jaiswal (1965), the only way to open up a new field of employment and it will ultimately bring prosperity in the rural areas to start large number of properly planned Agro Industries.

Manjumdar (1966) pointed out that the strategic importance of Agro processing industries started from the fact that backward linkage effect was important for agricultural growth and forward linkage effect provided the base for rural industrialisation.

Pillai (1972) in his study revealed that as many agricultural product had a parallel agro industry and showed that the crops like rice, jowar, ground nut, sugar cane, cotton etc. grown in Meerut dist. attracted as many as ten different industries.

Subramani and Potti (1976), pointed out that the production of food grains, oil seeds, fruits and vegetables, sugarcane would reach 187 MT, 135MT, 16.5MT, 48MT, 171MT respectively in 2000 AD, and hence there was vast opportunities for the industries based on the agricultural products.

Arora (1978) stated that nearly 2/3 of industry in India was agro based and was dependent on agriculture directly or indirectly. There fore the prosperity of agrobased industries and economic development of the rural sector were closely inter-linked.

Kahalon and Singh (1979) suggested that the development of agriculture alone did not bring out any significant improvement in productivity and output. So agrobased industries should be developed side by side with agriculture.

Austin (1981) categorised agro industries into three stages on the basis of the degree of processing. He mentioned that higher degree of processing was accompanied by higher capital investment, technological complexity and higher value addition.

Ahluwalia and Rangarajan (1986) estimated that the dependence of the Indian industry on Agriculture was very high and added that growth of the industries was limited by the development of agriculture.

According to Swaminathan (1986), sustainability of rice production system had to be viewed with serious concern along with the sustainability of ecosystem, since other two factors viz. political and economic were highly controversial with arguments for and against. Ecological consideration was the main study, since one has to think about the survival of the future generation.

Srivastava (1989) divided Indian Agro Industry into Manual-mechanical, Mechanical, Chemical signifying higher degree of processing in that order. He observed some movement of agro-industries from mechanical based to chemical based processing and found mechanical-based processing dominates.

Singh and Vyasala (1989) highlighted the fact that there was a high degree of correlation between agriculture and agro based industries and as such, many economics of small scale fall to these industries.

Dixit (1991) stated that a continued economic growth could only be achieved through further value adding in agriculture. This study also mentioned that existing imbalance in the economy with 70 per cent of the population being supported by a sector contributing to only 40 per cent of the net domestic product, needs to be rectified.

Mohanty (1995) conducted a study on the impact of agro based industries on rural economy in Orissa and found that the agro based industries by raising income levels of the rural workers brought about significant changes in the standard of living which in term created a potential demand for goods and services. According to Sivayya and Das (1996) modernisation process should start at the base and this can be done only if we set up a chain of micro industries at the village level.

Study of Nair (1997) revealed that in Kerala, paddy fields are undergoing rapid conversion. As per revenue record in 1940, the area under wet paddy land colloquially named as 'Nilaoms' was 5.75 lakh hectares. It shrunk to 3.3 lakh hectors by 1992-93. Out of this, 2.4 lakh hectors was lost for paddy cultivation. 61% was lost for growing annuals and perennial crops, 15% was used for non-agricultural use and 8% still remain as fallow.

Study conducted by Venkatesh, Ramesh and Varada raju (1997) where about drought in Bijapur districts of Karnataka. The results indicated that the district had undergone extreme drought condition due to the conversion of wet land into other cultivation purposes.

From the study of Veeramoni, Balasubramaniyan (1997) they found out that drought in the various places of Tamil Nadu was mainly due to the paddy filed conversion and modern cultivation practices.

Jaikumaran (1999) opined that conversion of paddy land to other cash crops as well as non-agricultural uses had severally affected paddy land eco-system, apart from serious set back in rice production. Conversion was to be stopped at any cost for the sustainability of rice production as well as restoration and maintenance of environmental harmony.

Singh and Nema (1999) in their study revealed that agro-processing units operating in the area employed 2713 regular workers and 4739 casual labourers in the mustard oil seed processing while rice and pulses processing units jointly employed annually 2345 regular workers and 3331 casual labourers in this activity.

Ramiah (1937) in his study observed that Rice (*Oryaza sativa*) was one of the earliest crops which come under cultivation and it belonged to the great group of plant comprising the family of "GRAMINEAE" in which Wheat, Maize, Cholam, Ragi, Sugarcane and all fodder grasses were included.

Grist (1953) in his book discussed the evolution of rice, the evolution of rice certainly dates to the earliest age of man, and long before the era of which had historical evidence, the rice was probably the staple food and first cultivated crop in Asia.

Choudhary and Ghose (1953) stated that carbonized paddy grains were found in the excavations at Hastinapur (UP) at a site dated between 1000–750BC. This was the oldest rice specimen yet known in the world.

Richaria and Govinda Sami (1966) stated that Rice Research in India started only a half century ago in the province of Bengal by Dr. G. P. Hector in 1911 and by Dr. F. R. Parvell in Madras in the year 1912.

Comhaire (1965) in his book revealed that the demographic growth was no compensated for by an improvement of the yield of crops, the nutritional standard was very low and they lived permanently in danger of starvation. He identified the remedy for this was only increasing the area of rice field but also adopting modern and rational methods of cultivation.

Johnson (1969) in his study found that the need for planning for tackling marketing problem, viz. harvesting, transporting and processing became imperative in the situation created by the increased production of paddy.

Muthiah (1972) reported that there was a sharp rise in the production of paddy in South India in the wake of successful implementation of high yielding varieties programme between 1967–68 and 1970–71.

Sahadevan (1966) analysed the origin of the term and found that the generic name "oryaza" was derived from Arabic "Arruz" (Al-ruzz) which has its origin in the Dravidian name "Arsi" of which the Malayalam word "Ari" for rice was derived. He stated that Rice was predominantly an Asian crop, 60 per cent of its production and consumption being confined to the Asian countries.

Gai Kwad and Gupta (1979) in their study stated that paddy-rice system consisted of large number of process and activities and it started from post harvest process such as threshing, scalping, cleaning, separation, drying, parboiling, shelling, polishing, grading, packing, by-product utilization, marketing and to the consumer distribution.

Richaria (1966) identified different varieties of rice in India in a historic perspective. He stated that during the Vedic period their existed 400,000 varieties of rice and he estimated that there were 200,000 varieties are still existed in India. The study high lighted the fact that even if a person were to eat a new variety everyday of the year, he could live for over 500 years without re-using a variety. He further stated that 20,000 varieties of rice were collected and identified in the Chathisgarh area alone.

Randhawa (1980) examined that in later Vedic texts (1000–500 BC) there were reference to cultivation of wide range of cereals, vegetables fruits and use of iron implements. More over ploughing the soil, several times in a year, broad casting seed following and using of cow dung as a manure were stated, irrigation practices, operations of raping, threshing and winnowing were also described in the Vedic texts.

De Datta (1981) stated that some people in Indonesia believed that the rice grain had a soul like human being. In Srilanka Astrologers were often consulted and prayers offered before rice was planted.

Swaminathan (1985) stated that during the last 35 years, rice production in India had increased by 300 per cent from about 20MT in 1950 to nearly 60MT during 1983 - 84. According to him rice had been cultivating in India for the last 7000 years.

According to Mukherjee (1985) the study of market development for rice had received very little attention, this was due to production of rice being consistently below the market demand in India. According to him with the innovations of paddy-production technology, rice production exceeded the local demand in certain parts of the country and this necessitated the initiating of studies of market development of rice.

Murthy (1987) examined the trend in rice production, According to him the rice production was 39.3 million tonnes in 1964–65 and it increased to 58.6 MT in 1984–85. He also stated that productivity increased from 1.07 to 1.46 Tonnes/hectare during the same period.

Kant (1993) pointed out that the vast biomass that we produced in paddy cultivation is largely under utilized. According to him paddy husk and bran had immense potential for production of energy, edible oil, and several important chemicals with considerable value addition. He stated the need for promotion of modern paddy processing units on a large scale, to boost our processing industry.

Siddique (1994) examined the reasons for low rice export inspite of its vast potential. He urged that most modern automated rice mills were being set up, technology for making silky rice and colour sorters, automatic removal of red, discoloured and imperfectly polished kernels being introduced increasing number of export housed going for the ISO 9000 certificates innovations in packaging and other market strategies were to be given importance. Anitha (1995) in the study discussed the decline of rice cultivation in Kerala. The total geographical area of Kerala is 38.9 lakh hectares which is about 1.18 per cent of the total geographical area of the country. She identified that the state income during 1993-94 was Rs. 18133.44 crores, out of which the share of agriculture was estimated as Rs. 6102.18 crores which was about 33.65 per cent. She pointed out that rice cultivation declined because of low profitability and due to small size holdings. The average size of holding was only 0.31/ha/person.

Puntambaker (1994) stated that one job was created for every Rs. 5000/- investment in processing units besides other in allied activities like rawmaterial procurement, transportation, storage packing etc. According to him the capital out put ratio was very much favourable in the case of agro processing units.

Solvent Extractors Association (SEA) (1998) observed that India was facing a shortage edible oil, according to them Rice Bran Oil was the best Source of edible oil, it was a better cooking medium, Now India produces only 82 lakh Tonnes, with a potential to produce over 91 lakh Tonnes per annum. If the huller mills were modernized, the quality of bran can be improved and India can improve the production of rice bran oil also.

Vadivel (1999) stated that in India 100 million paddy was produced annually. About 10 per cent (10 million) was used for seed purpose, the balance paddy was processed and consumed as raw or parboiled rice, which was consumed in the country itself, and the international trade of rice was only 6.6 per cent of the total world's production.

Dawe (2000) pointed out that rice was one of the most important crops in terms of economic value and approximately 90 per cent of the world rice was grown and consumed in Asia in a belt ranging from Pakistan in the west to Japan in the east.

Singh and Pradmankumar (2002) observed that India had high population pressure on land. The massive increase in population and substantial income growth demand an extra 2.5 million tonnes of food grains annually. They estimated that the demand for food grains in the year 2007 will be at the level of 222 million Tonnes comprising 97 million Tonnes of Rice. Sujit and Sujikumar Mishra (2002) expressed belief that the concept of globalisation and liberalization encouraged the establishment of agro-processing industries in India. According to them the processed or value added rice products had large export potential.

Journal of Tropical Agriculture (2002) examined in Kerala there was a reduction of area under rice from 8.74 lakh ha in 1972–73 to 4.2 lakh ha in 1997–98. They have the opinion that due to various socio, economic, constraints a change of bringing more area under rice cultivation was very remote. Hence to achieve the target of increased rice production, it required raising productivity per Hector.

Sekhon, Rangi and Manjeer Kaur (2003) pointed out that the agro processing industries in India accounted for 19 per cent of the total industrial out put and provided employment to the extent of 19 per cent of the total industrial work force and accounted for 18 per cent of Gross National Product (GNP). According to them among agro-industries, rice processing industry was the biggest industry in India.

Shukla, Sharma, Krishna Murari (2003) in their study stated that rice was grown on 44.90 million hectors representing 33.2 per cent of the world rice acrege and 29.2 per cent of worlds rice production. Rice and Rice products earned a foreign exchange to the tune of Rs. 13 billion per annum through export. It also pointed out that the productivity of Indian rice during 1999-2000 was 1950/Kg/ha against world average of 3845 Kg/ha.

Balamurugan (2004) in his study stated that rice reflected our culture and unity. Value addition provides good market for agricultural products. He argued for sustainable agriculture as production of sufficient food grains for the present as well as future generation without altering the quality of soil.

According to Rice India Journal (2004) 'Rice is life' and it was a symbol of cultural identity and global unity. According to them rice shaped the religious observances, festivals, customs, cuisine and celebrations. Rice cultivation was the principle activity and sources of income for about 100 million house holds in Asia and Africa. They estimated that about four fifth of the world rice was produced by small scale farmers and was consumed locally.

RESEARCH GAP

Though some studies have already been conducted with regard to the general aspects of agro processing industry on the basis of survey of the available literature and discussion with the rice mill owners and rice traders. It was found that more serious and systematic studies are further needed in the field by analysing the performance of the rice mills in Kerala by concentrating in Ernakulam District. Earlier studies failed to cover different aspects such as the clustering of rice mills, financial performance capacity utilization, deceleration of rice production in Kerala and marketing strategy of the existing rice mill in Kalady cluster. The prospects for the rice- processing industry are growing day by day. No systematic study has been conducted so far regarding the important role of rice mills from the above mentioned lines. The present study is the culmination of a such a felt need and is the first of its kind in the field of agro-processing industry. An earnest and simple attempt is made to fill this research gap.

LIMITATIONS OF THE STUDY

Statistics relating to many aspects of the rice mills are scattered and inadequate. The rice mill business is an unorganized sector.

At present there is no government owned rice mill is operating in the state. So the data collection is a difficult job. Another limitation is that the study can be carried out from different angles such as from the point of view of owners, consumers, workers, and traders etc., the scope of the present study is limited to the analysis from the point of view of the rice mill owners and workers in and around Kalady. Due to the non-cooperation of respondents and partial disclosure of information by some of the rice mill owners, a census survey of the rice mills could not be carried out. Most of the primary data for the present study have been collected from sample respondents based on sample survey method.

In order to draw more meaningful and accurate inferences regarding the trends and composition of production, sales, marketing strategies etc. of rice mills in side the state, data for a fairly long period is required. The non-availability of reliable data is one of the serious limitation of the present study. This study is subject to the normal errors inherent to such social surveys due to the natural bias in the reporting of data by respondents. Even though utmost care has been taken in verifying the reliability of the data, the possibility of such errors cannot be completely be ruled out. Any other limitations in any part of this study is to be viewed not as arbitrary and deliberate.

CHAPTER SCHEME

The study is presented in six chapters. The first chapter is introductory chapter explaining the conceptual frame work, statement of the problem importance of the study, theoretical frame work, research gap objectives, hypotheses, scope and coverage analytical frame work and statistical tools, methodology, data sources, review of earlier studies, limitations and the design of the study.

The second chapter deals with the area, production and productivity of rice in India, Kerala and in Ernakulam Dist. Hence an explanation of land use pattern and trends in area and production under paddy cultivation is also attempted.

The third chapter presents a historical sketch of the rice mill business in Kerala and Kalady. The fourth chapter deals the history of the clustering of rice mills in an around Kalady and the influence of locational factors that result in the conglomeration of rice mills in Kalady in lines with Porter's Dimoned Model of Clustering.

The fifth chapter deals about the financial performance and problems of modern rice mills in Kalady.

The sixth chapter presents the Findings and Conclusions of the study and the Suggestions and Recommendations based on the findings of the study. This chapter also presents an enquiry into the possibility of further research in this field.

2

RICE ECONOMY OF KERALA

Rice, Oryaza sativa, belongs to the family of grasses, 'Gramineae', the most important family of plants comprising of wheat, maize, cholam, ragi, sugar cane, and all fodder grasses. The generic name 'Oryaza' derived from the Arabic, 'Arruzz' (Al-ruzz) which has its origin in the Dravidian name 'Arsi' of which the Malayalam word 'Ari' for rice is later derivation. The word Arsi in turn is considered to be derived from the original Malayalam word 'Erus'.

Rice is one of the earliest of the crops to come under cultivation. It is the main staple food of half the worlds population. Rice is a symbol of cultural identity and global unity. Rice is the world's most popular food. It is cultivated in 113 countries and provides 27 per cent of dietomy energy supply and 20 per cent dietomy protein intake. Paddy cultivation is the principal activity and source of income for about 100 million households in Asia and Africa. About 4/5 of the world's rice is produced by small scale farmers and consumed locally. So world trade in rice is less than 5 per cent of total production.

HISTORY OF RICE CULTIVATION

The term Agriculture is derived from the latin words 'ager' or 'agri' meaning soil and 'cultura' meaning cultivation. Agriculture is a very broad term encompassing all aspects of crop production, live stock farming, fisheries, forestry etc.

Table 1
Vernacular Names of Rice

Language	*Rough rice*	*Clean rice*
Malayalam	Nellu	Ari
Tamil	Nellu	Arisi
Canarese	Bhatta	Akki
Telugu	Odlne	Biyyam
Hindi	Dhan	Chaval
Bengali	Dhan	Chaul
Sanskrit	Kalama: Sali; Vreedhi	Tandula
English	Paddy	Rice
Arabic	Arruz	–
Greek	Oruza	–
French	Riz	–

Agronomy is a branch of agricultural science which deals with principles and practice of soil, water and crop management. This term is derived from Greek words 'agros' meaning field and 'nomos' meaning to manage.

The earliest man 'Homo Creetus' emerged around one and half million years ago and by about a million years ago, he spread throughout old world tropics and to later to temperate zones. About five hundred thousand years ago, he learned to control and use fire. The earliest man is distinguished from fellow animals by his intelligence and skill in making tools.

'Homo sapiens' the direct ancestor of modern man lived two hundred and fifty thousand years ago – Homo sapiens sapiens'. The modern man appeared in Africa about thirty five thousand years ago. He is distinguished from all other existing species of the 'Genus Homo' by large brain, small teeth and chin and capacity for making and using tools. He hunted variety of animals and cooked their meat on fire. The weapons for hunting were boulders and spears of wood tipped with blades of flint. He also used stone tipped arrows. Later, he domesticated the dog which greatly helped him in hunting. Apart from the meat of animals he gathered variety of seeds, leaves and fruits from the jungle.

It is estimated that most efficient hunting and gathering can hardly support one person per square kilometer while pastoral life can support three persons and agriculture about a hundred persons. He had no control over food supply and was unable to clothe and shelter adequately. During the period 8700 BC to 7700 BC he domesticated animals and turned a herds man. He first domesticated sheep and later goat. Between the period 7500 BC to 6500 BC, man gradually shifted from hunting and gathering to agriculture. Stones were used for cutting trees and fire for burning forests. Grains of cereals were dibbled with the aid of pointed sticks. Later on stone-hoes with wooden handles were invented. The cereals grown during this period were meat and barley and later rice, maize and millets. Subsequently he domesticated cattle, pigs, horses and ass.

Agriculture has no simple and single origin. It was started in different parts of the world during different periods. Present day agriculture in India as elsewhere has evolved itself through ages. As India was a pastoral country before agriculture was started, development of crops and animals took place concurrently leading to various types of farming systems that are now seen in different parts of the country.

India's most important contribution to world agriculture is rice, the staple food crop of most of South, South-East and East Asia. Sugar cane, number of legumes and tropical fruit like mango, are also natives of India. Indus valley and Harappa civilization flourished from the close of the third millennium BC. Excavations in this area revealed huge granaries. Barley, wheat, seasame, peas, date palm, cotton and textiles were the main crops during this period. Wooden plough and wheat carte were in use. Farmers used siling-balls for searing. Harappens were aware of spinning and weaving of cotton into cloth.

In later Vedic texts (1000-500 BC) there are references to cultivation of a wide range of cereals, vegetables, fruits and use of iron implements. Ploughing the soil several times, broadcasting seeds, fallowing and certain sequence of cropping is also mentioned. Cowdung was used as manure. Irrigation

Table 2
Important events in the History of Agriculture

Period	*Events*
Earlier than 10000 BC	Hunting, Gathering
8700 BC	Domestication of sheep
7700 BC	Domestication of Goat
7500 BC	Cultivation of wheat and barley
6000 BC	Domestication of Cattle and Pigs
4400 BC	Cultivation of maize
3500 BC	Cultivation of Potato
3400 BC	Invention of Wheel
3000 BC	Use of Bronze to make tools
2900 BC	Invention of plough, Irrigation in farming
2700 BC	Domesticatioin Silk-moth in China
2300 BC	Cultivation of chickpea, pear Sarson and cotton
2200 BC	Cultivation of Paddy (rice)
2200 BC	Domestication of fowl, buffalo and Elephant
1800 BC	Cultivation of finger millet (Ragi)
1725 BC	Cultivation of Sorghum
1700 BC	Taming of horse
1500 BC	Cultivation of Sugar cane, invention of wells.
1400 BC	Use of iron
15th centaury AD	Cultivation of sweet orange, sour orange, wild brinjal, Pome granate
16th century AD	Introduction of several crops into India by Portuguese: Potato, sweet arrowroot, cassane, Tomato, ehillies, pumpkin, Papaya, Pineapple, guava, custardapple, ground nut, cashewnut, Tobacco, American cotton, rubber.

Source: "A History of Agriculture in India, Vol. I & II by Randhawa M.S. (1980)

of crops was common. Operations of harvesting threshing and winnowing are also described in Vedic texts. Monumental irrigation works were executed as early as first century AD.

RICE : A WORLD SCENARIO

Rice, though principally a tropical crop requiring high temperature and humidity for its growth, is cultivated both in the tropical and subtropical areas extending from 40° South to 45° North of latitude. However most of the rice producing area lies between equator 40° North and between 70° to 140°E longitude. It occupies 256 million acres, with an average annual production of about 116 million tonnes of clean rice.

GEOGRAPHICAL CONDITIONS

Climate : Rice requires very hot and humid conditions. As such it thrives in areas of high temperature and heavy rain fail. During the growing season temperature should not be less than 75°F. There should also be much water both in and upon the soil. Average annual rainfall varying from 40" to 60" is required for successful cultivation of rice. In areas with less than 40" of rainfall, rice cultivation is hardly possible except with irrigation. For, the paddy plant requires swamp, moist conditions during the period of its growth: it is ideal if the fields get flooded. During the ripening period a hot, dry climate is desirable.

Soil: Rice is grown on a variety of soils such as alluvial soil, red soil, black soil, clayey soil etc. Soil with a light loam on the surface to allow root development and a heavy clayey layer a short distance below the surface soil to retain water at the root is considered to be most ideal for rice cultivation. Rice requires extremely level land so that water will remain stagnant during the growing season-upland or hill rice can be grown on hill slopes, but the bulk of rice grown in the world is lowland or swamp rice, which requires level or flooded fields. The largest rice growing area as of the world are the river basis, deltas and coastal plains situated with in the tropics.

RICE PRODUCING COUNTRIES IN THE WORLD

Rice is grown on all the continents of the world. As a global food, it has a large influence on human nutrition and food security all over the world. Rice is a crop of the tropical regions especially of the monsoon lands. As such the important rice growing areas of the world are situated in Asia, where the monsoon is most predominant. Monsoon lands of Asia satisfy not only the climatic and soil conditions but also have a large supply of cheap labour, which is essential for rice cultivation. About 90 per cent of the world's rice is grown in Asia. The important rice producing countries of Asia are China, India,

Burma, Malaysia, Pakistan, Vietnam, Indonesia, Thailand, Korea, Formosa, Japan, Srilanka, Laos, Combodia and Philippines. China is the largest producer of rice and India ranks second.

Non-Asian countries producing rice include Egypt (UAR) Italy, Spain, Yugoslavia, U.S.A., Brazil and Australia. Owing to climatic limitations Europe produces only about 0.5 per cent of the world production. U.S.A. produces on an average 6 million metric tonnes of rice, annually.

Table 2a
Countries Producing, Consuming, Exporting and Importing Rice

Major Rice Producing countries	*Major consuming Countries*	*Major Exporting Countries*
China	China	Thailand
India	India	Vietnam
Indonesia	Indonesia	United States
Vietnam	Bangladesh	India
Bangladesh	Vietnam	China
Thailand	Burma	Pakistan
Burma	Japan	Uruguay
Brazil	Thailand	Australia
Japan	Brazil	Argentina
Philippines	Philippines	Guyana
United States	Korea South	Burma
Pakistan	United States	Iran
Korea-South	Egypt	
Egypt		
Taiwan		Korea North
Australia		Taiwan
Indonesia		South Africa
		China
Bangladesh		India
Philippines		Indonesia
Brazil		Philippines
Nigeria		United States
Saudi Arabia		Kenia South
Japan		Thailand
Iraq		Brazil
Iran		Pakistan
Burma		
Malaysia		
Senegal		
Cote d'Ivories		
South Africa		

Contd...

Major Rice Producing countries	*Major consuming Countries*	*Major Exporting Countries*
Cuba		
Singapore		
Mexico		
Guinea		
Korea North		
Russia		
United States		
Turkey		
Canada		
Eastern Europe		
Haiti		
China		
Peru		
Syria		
Colombia		
Ghana		
Srilanka		
Yemen		
Jordan		
Korea South		
UAE		
Costa Rica		
Jamica		

Source: India grains, Vol. 1, No. 4, August 1999.

The Table 3 shows India has the largest area of cultivation followed by China and Indonesia. Australia, Japan and Republic of Korea rank first in the area of irrigated land. China

Table 3
Distribution of Rice Area in Selected Countries

Country	*Rice Area (000ha)*	*Distribution of Rice Area in %*			
		Irrigated	*Rainfed*	*Flood prone*	*Upland*
India	42649	43.0	30.1	11.4	14.6
China	33019	92.7	5.6	00	1.7
Indonesia	10282	72.0	7.8	6.4	13.8
Japan	2049	99.0	00	00	1.0
Republic of korea	1208	99.0	00	00	1.0
Egypt	462	100	00	00	00
Australia	89	100	00	00	00
USA	1123	100	00	00	00

Source: IRRI Rice Almanac II Edition 1997.

has 92.7 per cent irrigated land but India has only 43.8 per cent. This also affects the productivity of paddy. India has the largest flood prone area, naturally rice cultivation in this area may be a gamble with monsoon.

Table 4
Area, Production and Productivity of Selected Rice Growing Countries

Country	*Area* 00ha	*Production* 000MT	*Productivity* Ton/Ha
India	44800	87904	1.96
China	31720	134334.3	4.23
Indonesia	11624	33187.7	2.85
Japan	1788	7684.2	4.29
Republic of Korea	1059	4871.5	4.60
Egypt	655	3896.7	5.95
USA	1442	6395.8	4.43
Australia	140	944.7	6.74

Source: FAO Year Book 1999.

Table 4 shows India has the largest area of rice cultivation but she is second to China in the production of rice. Egypt and Australia have the lowest area of rice cultivation. In India rice is grown mainly in monsoon climatic regions. Lack of infrastructure facilities such as irrigation, mechanization, fertilizers, non-application of HYV seeds etc. are the constraints in the low productivity of rice in India. Australia has only 140 thousand ha of rice field and about 100 per cent area is irrigated. She tops in the rice productivity as many important factors such as irrigation, mechanization, fertilizer application, use of HYV seeds etc. are very much being followed.

Table 5
Comparative Yield of Rice in Different Countries

Country	*Productivity/ha (kg)*
India	1994
China	6321
Japan	6414
USA	6622
Indonesia	4261
Vietnam	4105

Source: Statistics at a glance, Ministry of Agriculture GOI

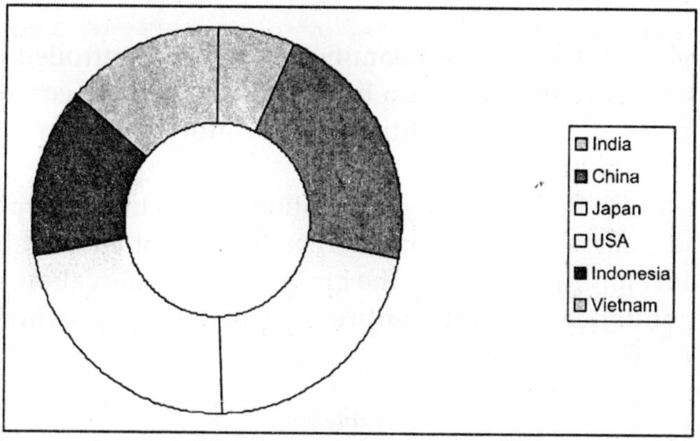

Figure 1: **Comparative Productivity of Rice in Different Countries**

RICE PRODUCTION IN INDIA: AN ANALYSIS

Rice is the most important crop and it occupies the largest area in the Indian Union, and she is the second largest producer in the world next only to China. India has appropriate varieties and vast under utilized potential to meet the growing demand of rice. Rice is grown in almost all the states of India, but its cultivation is mostly concentrated in the river valleys, deltas, and low lying coastal areas of North-Eastern and Southern India, comprising the States of Andhrapradesh, Tamil Nadu, Karnataka, Kerala, Assam, Bihar, Maharashtra, Madhya Pradesh, Orissa, Chathisgarh, Uttar Pradesh and West Bengal. The growth of rice production since independence has been impressive in terms of volume of production. However, the dependence of climate is still a very dominant factor in most parts of the country because of the infrastructure facilities such as irrigation, electricity, fertilizer, transportation etc. have not been developed to the required level. Even now a bad monsoon drastically alters the production of rice and socio-economic condition of farmers. There are other factors, which do have significant impact on rice production like land holding, seeds, fertilizers, irrigation and many more. The factors that determine production can be categorized in to two ways as controlled factors and uncontrolled factors. Land holding, fertilizer use, seeds and technology are controlled one, whereas rainfall, naturalcalamities etc. are uncontrolled ones. Shortage of rainfall can also be termed as partially controlled factors as irrigation facilities could nullify the shortage of rainfall to a great extent.

In India food security as a national objective was placed on the policy agenda much earlier than in other developed and developing countries. The growth of rice cultivation, since independence has been impressive in terms of volume of production.

Table 6
Area and Production of Rice in British Provinces

	Area of Production (000 acres)		*Production (000 Tons)*	
States	*Year*	*Year*	*Year*	*Year*
	1977-26	1927-30	1922-26	1927-30
Assam	4487	4554	1527	1464
Bengal	20793	20604	7968	8615
Bihar and Orissa	14446	14015	4636	5466
Bombay including Sindh	3068	3142	1355	1372
Burma	11996	12691	4739	4818
Central province	5193	5486	1460	1605
Madras	10968	11285	4947	5259
United Province	7178	6902	2168	1709
Total	78129	78679	28800	30308

Source: Ministry of Agriculture and Fisheries England Imperial Council of Agricultural Research (K. Ramiah, 1937).

During 1922-26 rice was cultivated in only 78129 thousand Acres and produced 28800 thousand tonnes during 1927-30, there was a slight expansion of area under cultivation which in turm increased the area to 78679 thousand Acres of land and produced 30308 thousand Tonnes of rice. The per capita production of rice was as low as 50 gms.

The above table shows that after independence, the per capita availability of food grains especially rice per day and wheat per day is showing an increasing trend. During and after independence period the per capita rice availability was only 58 gm/day against 73.8 gm/day. Food grains/day

Table 7
Percapita availability of Rice in India

(Grams per day)

Year	*Rice*	*Wheat*	*Cereals*	*Pulses*	*Food grains*
1951	58.0	24.0	334.4	60.7	394.9
1961	73.4	28.9	399.7	69.0	468.7
1971	70.3	37.8	417.6	51.2	468.8
1981	72.2	47.3	417.3	37.5	454.8
1991	80.9	60.0	468.2	41.6	510.1
2001	73.8	56.9	433.7	36.7	470.4

Source: Economic Survey 2001.

availability was also increased from 394.9 gm/day to 470.4/ gm/day during 2001. This figures show the remarkable progress achieved by India after a period of 50 years. Now India is self sufficient in food grains.

Table 8
The Gross Cropped Area Under Various Crops in the Country

(Area million ha)

Crop	*1950-51*	*1960-61*	*1980-81*	*1990-91*	*1998-99*
Total Cropped Area (Gross cropped Area)	131.89	152.77	172.63	185.74	192.62
Rice	30.81	34.13	40.15	42.69	44.80
	(23.26)	(22.34	(23.26)	(22.98)	(23.26)
Wheat	9.75	12.93	22.28	24.17	27.52
	(7.39)	(8.46)	(12.91)	(13.01)	(14.29)
Coarse Cereals	37.67	44.96	41.78	36.32	29.34
	(28.56)	(29.43)	(24.20)	(19.55)	(15.23)
Pulses	19.09	23.56	22.46	24.66	22.87
	(14.47)	(15.42)	(13.01)	(13.28)	(1.87)
Oilseeds	10.73	13.77	17.60	24.15	26.23
	(8.14)	(9.01)	(10.19)	(13.00)	(13.62)
Cotton	5.88	7.01	7.82	7.44	9.34
	(4.46)	(4.98)	(4.53)	(4.01)	(4.85)
Sugar Cane	1.71	2.42	2.67	3.69	4.05
	(1.30)	(1.59)	(1.55)	1.99)	(2.10)
Potato	0.24	6.38	0.73	0.94	1.32
	(0.18)	(0.25)	0.43)	(0.51)	(0.68)

Note: figures in brackets denote percentages
Source: Government of India, Office of Agriculture Commissioner July 2003.

Table 8 shows that the gross cropped area has increased to 40 million ha over the period of last 40 years. However, there has been differential behaviour in this increase. Of the total increase, rice and wheat alone account for 25.26 million ha while oil seeds account for 12.46 million ha. The area under pulses has been almost constant over decades. (22.23 million ha) while that of coarse cereals has reduced by 15.62 million ha.

An overall analysis of the data in Table 2.8 indicates that the present area under rice has been almost constant (22-23 per cent) over the years. Area under wheat has increased from 7.38 per cent in 1950-51 to 14.29 per cent in 1998-99. Area under rice cultivation has been increased from 30.81 lakh ha to 44.80 lakh ha in 1998-99. The total cropped area also shows increasing trend. The total cropped area of 131.89 lakh ha in 1950-51 has increased to 192.62 lakh ha., by 1998-99. It was 192.62 lakh ha, about 61 lakh ha of further land were utilized for agricultural purposes. The production of food grains was also increased to a large extend and India attained self sufficiency in food grains. This can definitely be considered as a remarkable achievement.

Table 9
India's Population and its growth from 1901 to 2001

Census year	*Population (in lakhs)*	*Decadal growth Rate*
1901	2383.9	–
1911	2520.9	5.75
1921	2513.2	0.31
1931	2789.8	11.00
1941	3186.6	14.22
1951	3610.9	13.31
1961	4392.3	21.64
1971	5481.6	24.80
1981	6833.3	24.66
1991	8433.9	23.86
2001	10270.2	21.34

Source: Census Reports GOI

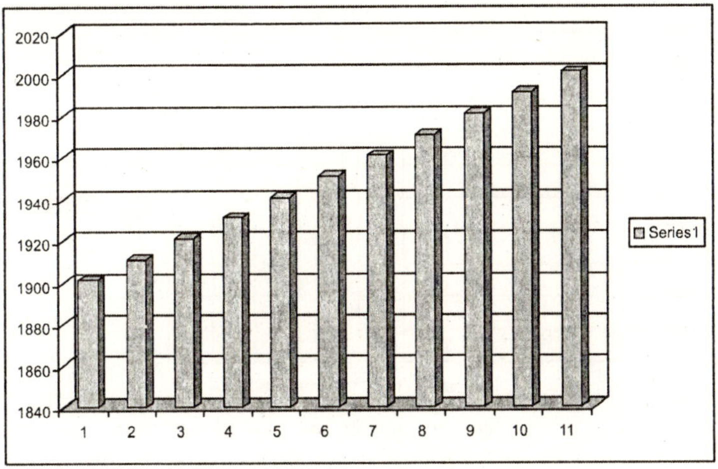

Figure 2: **Population of India from 1901 to 2001**

As per 1951 census report, India had more than 36 crores of people and population increased to 103 crores by 2001. Between a period of 50 years population was increased about 67 crores increased in population with in a period of 50 years point to the urgent need to find out ways and means to support the increasing population in India especially the food one requirements.

Table 10

Area Under Rice Cultivation in India, in Different Years

Year	*Area (000 ha)*
1950-51	30811
1955-56	31521
1960-61	34255
1965-66	35273
1970-71	37592
1975-76	39475
1980-81	40152
1985-86	41137
1990-91	42686
1995-96	42836
2000-01	44710
2002-03	40410

Source : Ministry of Agriculture Task Force on field crops, CMIE 2000, Economic Review 2004.

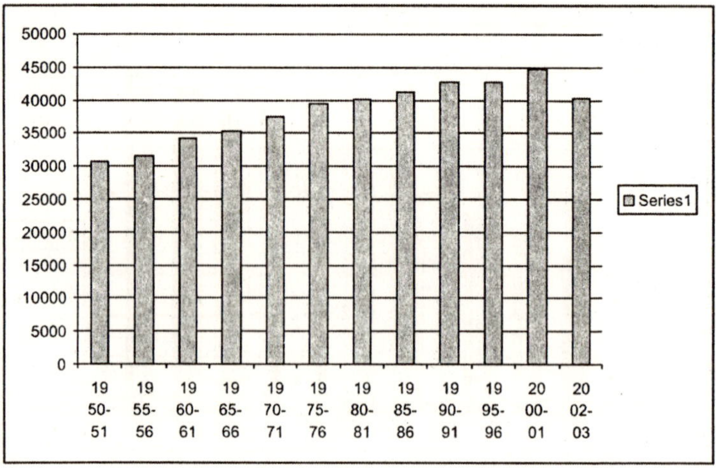

Figure 3: **Area Under Rice Cultivation in India**

Rice production in India substantially increased from 1970-71 to 2003-04. (Table 11). Increase in rice production was more essential to cop up with the tremendus increase in population in India, the second largest populated country in the world.

Table 11
Production of Rice in India

Year	*Production (000 MT)*
1970-71	42225
1975-76	48740
1980-81	53631
1985-86	63825
1990-91	74291
1995-96	76975
2000-01	84980
2001-02	93080
2002-03	75702
2003-04	87000

Source: Ministry of Agriculture, Task force on filed crops Economic Review and CMIE.

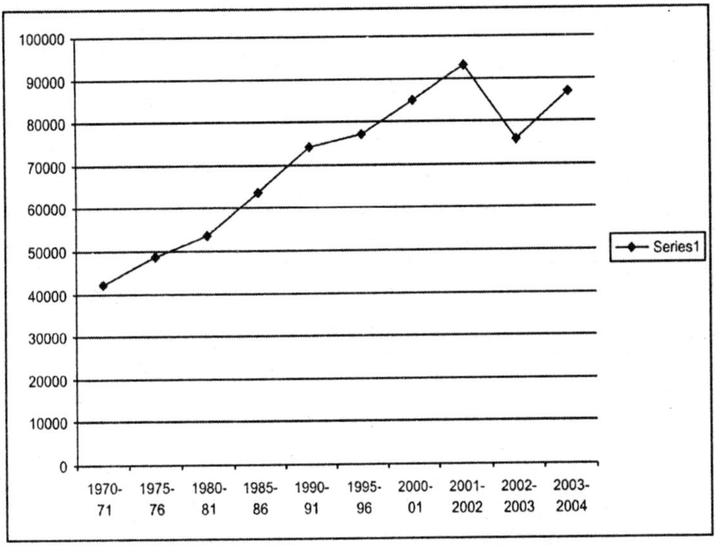

Figure 5: **Production of Rice in India**

During 1970-71 India's rice production was 42.225 lakh million tonnes but during 2003-04. It was 87 lakh million tonnes. This is because the area of production as well as productivity has also increased. The increase in rice production in India over the years is directly propotional to the increase in area under cultivaiton as well as productivity (Table 12).

Table 12
Productivity of Rice in India

Year	*Productivity (Kg/ha)*
1970-71	1123
1975-76	1235
1980-81	1336
1985-86	1552
1990-91	1740
1995-96	1797
2000-01	1901
2001-02	2086
2002-03	1874

Source: Ministry of Agriculture Task force on field crops Economic Review, CMIE.

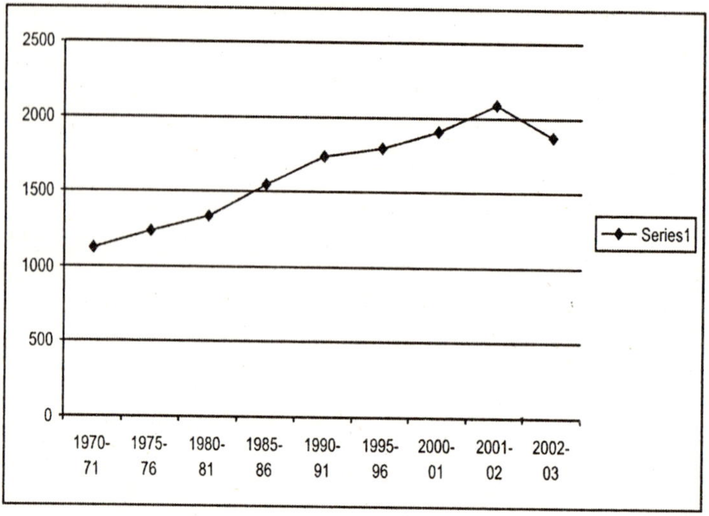

Figure 6: **Productivity of Rice in India**

Table 12 shows that the productivity of Rice has increasing from 1123 Kg/ha to 2086 Kg/ha in 2001-02. This is a positive symptom even though the world average of rice is much more than this. The advent of high yielding varieties, modern production technologies coupled with adequate use of plant nutrient and better management of inputs increased the rice production from 20 million tones in 1950-51 to 84980 million tonnes in 2000.01. The average productivity of rice in India during 2001-02 was 2086 kg/ha against world average of 3845 kg/ha. The productivity within India varies with different agro-climatic zones/areas (Table 13).

Table 13 shows almost all the states in India showed an increasing trend in area of cultivation except Kerala. States like Gujarat, Jammu and Kashmir, Haryana etc. showed very positive trend, the area of cultivation is increasing. Uttar Pradesh ranks first in area of cultivation followed by West Bengal and Bihar. Punjab has a very positive trend, it almost doubled its area of cultivation within a period of 18 years.

Table 13
Area Under Cultivation of Rice in Different States of India

Area (000 ha)

States	*1980-81*	*1997-98*	*1998-99*
Andhra Pradesh	3600.3	3500.8	4120
Assam	2275	2489.8	2420.1
Bihar	5550.7	4975.5	5099.9
Gujarat	477.5	672.5	622.1
Haryana	472.0	910.0	1083.0
Jammu & Kashmir	265.0	275.7	270.3
Karnataka	1101.0	1378.2	1425.5
Kerala	802.0	404.1	348.2
Madhya Pradesh	4860.0	5403.4	5305.2
Maharastra	1504.0	1476.9	1483.1
Orissa	4191.0	4496	4447
Punjab	1178.0	2279	2519
Rajasthan	170.0	163.4	168
Tamil Nadu	2230	2361	2386.4
Uttar Pradesh	5292.0	5663.5	5932.3
West Bengal	5176	5900.2	5904.1
All India	40152.0	43420.2	44597.7

Source: CMIE.

Table 14
Production of Rice in Different States of India

(Production 000 tonnes)

States	*1980-81*	*1997-98*	*1998-99*
Andhra Pradesh	7011.4	8510	11434
Assam	2523	3382.9	3254.8
Bihar	5635.1	6774.9	6632.5
Gujarat	556.6	1042.3	1015.8
Haryana	1228.0	2545.0	2425.0
Jammu & Kashmir	547.0	549.3	589.1
Karnataka	2208	3334.3	3604.5
Kerala	1272.0	661.0	658.6
Madhya Pradesh	4053.0	4488	5373.9
Maharastra	2361	2394.6	2467.6
Orissa	4301	6204.6	5391.5
Punjab	3223	7897.0	7940.0
Rajasthan	150.0	190.2	205.4
Tamil Nadu	4159.0	7052.0	8115.3
Uttar Pradesh	5570.0	12163.4	11615.9
West Bengal	7466.0	13236.5	13316.5
All India	53631.0	82299.7	85994.5

Source: CMIE.

Table 14 shows that West Bengal is the largest producer of rice, followed by Uttar Pradesh. The states like Punjab, Tamil Nadu showed very positive signals of increased production. Kerala showed very discouraging trend as its production was decreasing year by year.

Table 15
Productivity of Rice in different States

(Productivity Kg/ha)

States	*1980-81*	*1997-98*	*1998-99*	*2001-02*
Andhra Pradesh	1950	2431	2780	2978
Assam	1110	1359	1340	NA
Bihar	1020	1362	1300	NA
Gujarat	1170	1550	1630	NA
Haryana	2600	2797	2240	NA
Jammu & Kashmir	2060	1992	2180	NA
Karnataka	2010	2419	2530	NA
Kerala	1590	1636	1890	2218
Madhya Pradesh	830	831	1010	NA
Maharastra	1570	1621	1660	NA
Orissa	1030	1380	1210	NA
Punjab	2740	3465	3150	3545
Rajasthan	880	1164	1220	NA
Tamil Nadu	1870	2987	3440	3263
Uttar Pradesh	1050	2148	1960	2120
West Bengal	1440	2243	2260	2514
All India	1340	1895	1930	2086

Source: CMIE and Economic Review 2003.

Table 15 shows the productivity of rice in different states High productivity may be attributed to different factors such as the use of HYV seeds, use of fertilizers, pesticides, irrigation facilities, transportation and mechanization. The states which which followed modern scientific cultivation practices showed high productivity. The states like Punjab, Haryana, Tamil Nadu etc. are following the scientific cultivation practices for increasing productivity. The average productivity of rice in India during 1999-2000 was 1950 kg/ha against world average of 3845 kg/ha. This variability in rice yield also exist with in the country depending on agro climatic conditions. The average productivity of rice during 1998-99 in Orissa, Assam, Bihar was 1210, 1340 and 1300 kg/ha respectively as compared to 2780, 3150, 3440 kg/ha in Andhra Pradesh, Punjab and Tamil Nadu respectively. The wide variation in productivity among the states appears major cause for slow growth in rice production in the country.

Table 16
Area under High Yielding Varieties of (HYV) Rice in India

Year	*Area Under HYV RiceMillion ha*	*% of HYV to otal Area*
1966-67	0.9	2.6
1989-90	26.2	62.1
1990-91	27.4	64.2
1991-92	28.0	65.7
1992-93	27.5	65.9
1993-94	28.9	68.8
1994-95	31.0	74.6

Table 16 shows that there is a tendency to cultivate HYV of rice as its productivity is very high and cost of cultivation is very moderate. By using the HYV the country can increase total production of rice and can save a huge amount since the cost of cultivation is low when compared to traditional varieties.

Table 17
Area under HYV of Rice in different States during 1996-97

States	*Area (000 ha)*	*Percentage to total cultivated Area*
Arunachal Pradesh	35	28.6
Assam	1422	57.1
Bihar	3500	69.0
Orissa	3027	67.8
West Bengal	4463	76.9
Manipur	72	43.3
Meghalaya	42	39.7
Mizoram	5	7.7
Nagaland	2	1.2
Sikkim	7	43.7
Tripura	223	
Haryana	515	62.0

Contd...

States	*Area (000 ha)*	*Percentage to total cultivated Area*
Jammu and Kashmir	276	100
Punjab	2041	94.5
Uttar Pradesh	5018	90.4
Andhra Pradesh	3699	93.2
Karnataka	1016	75.4
Tamil Nadu	2120	93.4
Gujarat	533	83.0
Madhya Pradesh	3471	65.6
Maharashtra	1293	87.5

Source: Fertilizer Statistics 2001.

Table 18
Cost and Returns of Rice Cultivation in Major Rice Producing States

Rs/ha

Year 1	*States* 2	*Total Income* 3	*Total Cost* 4	*Net Returns* 5
1995-96	Assam	8471	7888	583
	Orissa	11562	9842	1720
	West Bengal	14149	12215	1934
	Uttar Pradesh	14320	11301	1619
	Andhra Pradesh	19246	17980	1266
	Punjab	17799	15526	2273
	Maharashtra	10146	10307	161
1996-97	Assam	9050	8619	431
	Orissa	10310	10888	578
	West Bengal	14149	12215	1934
	Uttar Pradesh	NA	NA	NA
	Andhra Pradesh	22101	20937	1166
	Punjab	21158	17967	3191
	Maharashtra	NA	NA	NA
1997-98	Assam	10893	9502	1319
	Orissa	12757	11646	1111
	West Bengal	19806	18644	1162
	Uttarpradesh	NA	NA	NA
	Andhra Pradesh	20753	21040	287
	Punjab	23931	18993	4938

Source: Cost of cultivation principal crops in India, Directorates of Economics and Statistics, Ministry of Agriculture Government of India.

Table 18 indicates the cost of cultivation and returns indicate that the highest net return of Rs. 4939/ha in Punjab and the lowest in Orissa (Rs. 1111/ha) during 1997-98. This range of variation in farm income clearly indicates the factors responsible for backwardness of the traditional rice growing states. The net returns from rice cultivation is the highest in Punjab because they are using HYV seeds, irrigation facilities and mechanization. In Maharashtra and West Bengal, the total cost on paddy cultivation exceeds the total income from paddy cultivation, it causing loss to the farmers. This is not a positive symptom as the marginal and small farmers practicing rice cultivation may even shift to other crops which may result in food scarcity in the years to come.

RICE CULTIVATION IN KERALA

Rice, one of the oldest food crops, is the staple food of the people of Kerala where it has been under cultivation, as in other parts of South India, from very ancient times. Since rice is the major food crop of Kerala majority of farmers in the State are rice farmers. The prosperity of the people of Kerala is based on the performance of the rice crop and hence Kerala's economy is rice based.

Rice is cultivated throughout Kerala, It is cultivated in a diversity of conditions and probably no where else the crop is cultivated under such situations. It is cultivated in regions situated 3 meters below Mean Sea level (MSL) as in Kuttanad and at another, it is cultivated at an altitude of 1400 meters as in high ranges. It is cultivated in 3 to 4 meters depth of water as in the case of 'Kolappala' variety and contrastingly in uplands where there is no standing water. In different types of soil, rice is being cultivated in Kerala. There are different varieties of diverse agronomic characters and different methods of cultivation as there are different situations and conditions under which rice is cultivated. It is cultivated in all districts of the state. Rice producing areas of the state can be geographically classified in to 8 regions: Kuttanad, Onattukara, Pokkali, Laturate Midland, Plain areas (Malayoram), Palakkad, Chittoor and High ranges, of which Kuttanad and Palakkad are known as the rice bowls of Kerala. (Figure 7).

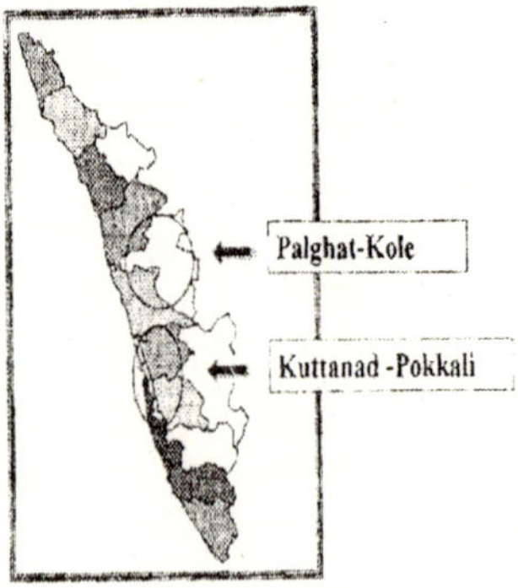

Figure 7

The area under rice cultivation during 1970 was increasing, but from 1980 it showed a decreasing trend. Rice production in Kerala showed a declining trend after 1970. The gap between demand and supply of grains which was around 50% till the mid seventies started widening there after consistent to the large scale shift in paddy lands for cultivation of other more remunerative crops like coconut, rubber, banana etc.

The area under rice cultivation in Kerala from 1955-56 to 2003-04. is presented in Table 19 and Figure 8.

Table 19
Trend of Area of Rice Cultivation in Kerala

Year	*Area (000 ha)*
1955-56	759.00
1960-61	778.940
1965-66	802.33
1970-71	874.93
1975.76	875.16
1980-81	854.37
1985-86	806.92
1990-91	559.45
1995-96	471.15
2000-01	347.455
2001-02	322.368
2002-03	310.521
2003-04	287.340

Source: Directorate of Economics and Statistics, Economic Review 2005.

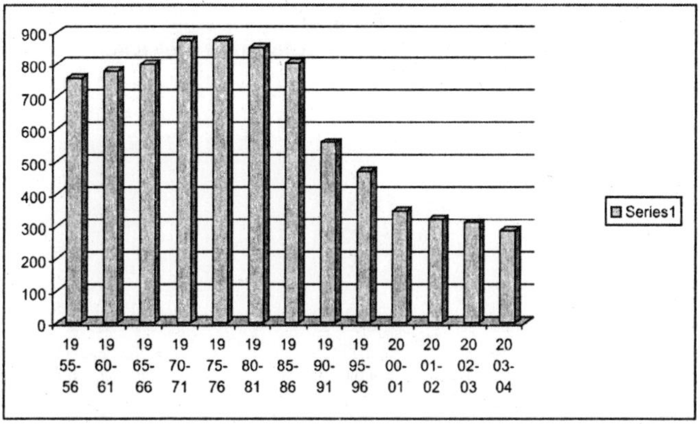

Figure 8: **Trend of Area of Rice Cultivation in Kerala**

There was a sharp decline in area of cultivation after 1980-81. During the year 1980-81 it was cultivated in an area of 854 000 ha, but during 2003-04 only it has decreased to 287 340 ha. Thus there was a tremendous decline of 567 000 ha during the period.

Table 20
Trends in Rice Cultivation in Kerala, from 1990-91 to 2003-04

Year 1	*Area (000 ha)* 2	*Change over previous years* 3	*Percentage changes* 4
1990-91	559	–	–
1991-92	541	18	3.22
1992-93	538	3	3.75
1993-94	507	31	9.30
1994-95	503	4	10.01
1995-96	471	32	17.53
1996-97	431	40	22.89
1997-98	387	44	30.59
1998-99	353	34	36.67
1999-2000	350	3	37.00
2000-01	348	2	37.56
2001-02	323	25	42.03
2002-03	310	13	44.36
2003-04	287	23	48.48

* Colum number 4 is computed.

Source: Directorate of Economics and Statistics, Government of Kerala 2005.

Table 21
Area under Rice Cultivation in India and Kerala

Area (000 ha)

Year	*India*	*Kerala*	*Percentage No. of area in Kerala (Out of Total Area and in India)*
1955-56	31521	759	2.40
1960-61	34255	779	2.27
1965-66	35273	802	2.27
1970-71	37592	874	2.32
1975-76	39475	875	2.22
1980-81	40152	854	2.12
1985-86	41137	807	1.96
1990-91	42686	559	1.30
1995-96	42836	471	1.09
2000-01	44710	347	0.78
2002-03	40410	310	0.76

Source: CMIE, Directorate of Economics and Statistics.

The area under rice cultivation in India gradually increased from 315.21 lakh ha in 1955 - 56' to 44710 lakh ha in 2000-01. But there was a slight decline of 4300 ha in 2002-03 compared to the area cultivated in 2000-01 though the area under rice cultivation in Kerala gradually increased from 1955-56 to 1975-76. Their was a declining trend thereafter. By 2002-03 it has tremebndously declined to 5,67,000ha compared to 1975-76 (Table 21).

Table 22
Annual Decline in Paddy Cultivation Area (ha) Over the Previous Year in Kerala

1998-99	*1999-00*	*2000-01*	*2001-02*	*2002-03*	*2003-04*
34491	2857	2319	25087	11847	23181

Source: Directorate Economics and Statistics, and UPASI.

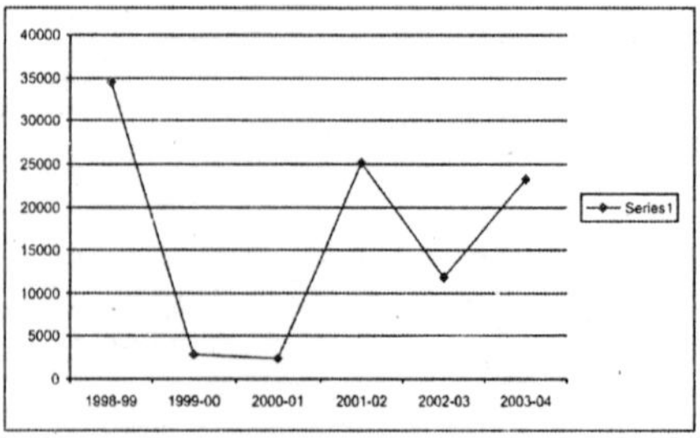

Figure 9: **Annual Decline in Paddy Cultivation Area (ha) over the Previous Years in Kerala**

The area and production of rice which were steadily increasing till the mid seventies had to succumb to economic pressure emanating from other remunerative crops like banana, coconut, rubber and the growth of the construction sector. This resulted in the decline of more than 5 lakh ha of area under paddy cultivation during the last two decades. The twenty five year period from mid seventies witnessed large scale shift in area under the crop. Rice production touched its peak level of around 14 lakh million tonns in mid seventies with a coverage of 8.81 lakh ha. The gap in meeting the internal demand of food grains was estimated to be 50 per cent during the period. The increasing cost of cultivation and the disproportionately small rise in price has acted a determent in rice production.

Table 23
Annual Foodgrain Requirement and Internal Production

(in lakh tonnes)

Year	*Food Grain requirement*	*Internal Production*	*Deficit*
1994	35.32	9.30	26.02
1995	35.76	8.60	27.16
1996	36.21	7.90	27.63
1997	36.64	7.90	28.74
1998	37.05	6.88	30.17
1999	37.40	6.54	30.86
2000	37.73	6.94	30.79
2001	38.04	6.76	31.28
2002	38.20	6.33	31.87
2003	38.78	6.42	32.36
2004	39.15	6.81	33.34

Source: Directorate of Civil Supplies, Government of Kerala.

Table 23 shows that annual foodgrain requiremnet and internal produciton. It is evident form the table that the foodgrain production is declining everyear and consequently the deficit is increasing. There is a wide gap between Demand and Supply of food grain requirement creates a serious threat to Kerala's food security.

Table 24
Production of Rice in Kerala

Year	*Production (000 tons)*
1956-57	887170
1960-61	106753
1965-66	99749
1970-71	129201
1972-73	137637
1975-76	133119
1980-81	1271362
1985-86	1173051
1990-91	1086578
1995-96	953026
2000-01	751328
2001-02	703504
2002-03	688859
2003-04	570045

Source: Economic Review 2005.

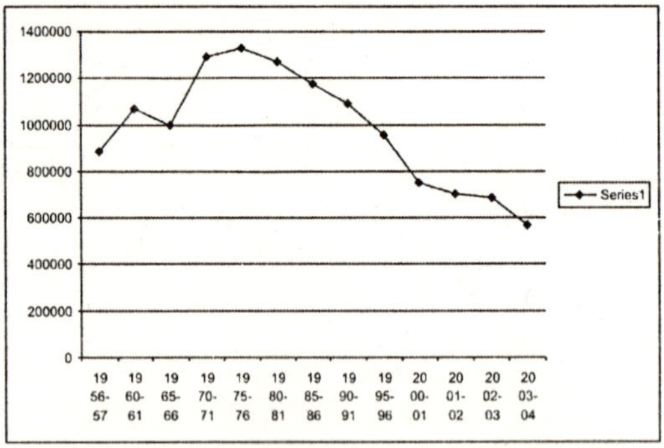

Figure 10: **Production of Rice in Kerala**

Table 24 shows the trend of production of rice in Kerala State. From this table it is evident that during 70's there was a trend of increasing production and set a record production of 1376370 MT in 1972-73 and in the beginning of 1985-86 onwards there was a decreasing trend and in the year 2003-04 it produced only 570045 M Tonnes of Rice which was only 30% of the total requirement Kerala requires to support its increasing population 38 million Tonnes of Rice for a year. As the population increases, naturally the food requirement was also increased.

Table 25
Production of Rice in India and Kerala

			Rice Production (in lakhs Tonnes)
Year	*India*	*Kerala*	*% of production in Kerala out of total production*
2	3	4	5
1992-93	72867	1085	1.49
1993-94	80298	1004	1.25
1994-95	81814	975	1.19
1995-96	76975	953	1.24
1996-97	81737	871	1.06
1997-98	82535	765	0.92
1998-99	85995	727	0.85
1999-2000	896980	771	0.085
2000-01	84871	751	0.88
2001-02	93080	704	0.76
2002-03	757020	689	0.91
2003-04	87000	570	0.66

* Column No. 5 are computed

Source: Directorate Economics and Statistics: Economic Review

Table 26
Trends in Production of Rice in Kerala

Year	*Production (Tones)*	*Change over Previous*	*Percentage of change year*
1990-91	1086588	2	1991-92
	1060370	-26218	-2.41
1992-93	1084878	24508	2.31
1993-94	1003938	-80940	-7.46
1994-95	975065	-28873	-2.88
1995-96	953026	-22039	-2.26
1996-97	871461	-81565	-8.56
1997-98	764610	-106851	-12.26
1998-99	726743	-37867	-4.95
1999-00	770686	43943	6.04
2000-01	751328	-19358	-2.51
2001-02	703504	-47824	-6.36
2002-03	688859	-14645	-2.08
2003-04	570045	-118814	-17.25

* Figures in column 4 and 5 are computed

Source: Directorate of Economics and Statistics: Economic Review GOI, CMIE

Since area under rice cultivation has decreased, a decline trend is also registered in the production. Total production of rice from 1991-2004 is exhibited in Table 26.

The production of rice from 1981 to 2004 showed a sharp declining trend in all the 14 districts of Kerala. The sharp reduction is more pronounced in the districts of Malappuram, Kozhikode, Alappuzha, Thrissur, Kannur, Palakkad and Ernakulam.

Figure 11: **Rice Cultivating areas of India**

Table 27
Productivity of Rice in Kerala Kg/ha

Year	*Productivity (Kg/ha)*
1955-56	1164
1960-61	1371
1965-66	1246
1970-71	1477
1975-76	1520
1980-81	1587
1985-86	1729
1990-91	1942
1995-96	2023
2000-01	2162
2001-02	2182
2002-03	2218
2003-04	1984

Source: Dept. of Economics & Statistics, Economic Review.

The trend in Productivity showed an increase in 1960-61 than in 1955-56 and there was a decline in the year 1965-66. Further their was an increase in 1970-71 and continued till 2002-2003. In the year 2003-2004 there was a fall in productivity because of the reduction in area was more during the Virippu Season when the productivity of the crop was generally higher than 'Mundakan' Season. The 'punja' crop, which was largely confined to the single cropped areas of Kuttanad and Kole areas was severely affected by the flood situation and resulted in crop failure.

Table 28
Productivity of Rice in Kerala and India

Year	*Productivity Kg/ha*	
	Kerala	*India*
1993-94	1977	1890
1994-95	1937	1910
1995-96	2023	1800
1996-97	2023	1882
1997-98	1975	1900
1998-99	2061	1930
1999-00	2203	1994
2000-01	2162	1913
2001-02	2182	2086
2002-03	2218	1874
2003-04	1984	2050

Source: Directorate of Economics and Statistics, GOK.

Table 28 Shows the productivity of Kerala and India. When compared to the national average the position of Kerala was better. But when compared to other states like Punjab, Andra Pradesh, Tamil Nadu etc, the production of Kerala was very low. The area of rice production in Kerala is decreasing year by year and this can be compensated to a small extent by increasing the productivity of rice. For this, application of High Yielding Variety Seeds, better infrastructure facilities etc are highly necessary.

Table 29
Productivity of HYV Rice in Kerala (1990-91 to 2003-04)

Year	*Productivity (Kg/ha)*
1990-91	2207
1991-92	2129
1992-93	2223
1993-94	2157
1994-95	2019
1995-96	2362
1996-97	2185
1997-98	2117
1998-99	2226
1999-00	2379
2000-01	2327
2001-02	2333
2002-03	2342
2003-04	2050

Source: Directorate of Economics and Statistics.

Table 29 shows the productivity of HYV rice from 1990-91 to 2003-04. The productivity of HYV rice in Kerala was not steady from 1990-91 to 1997-98. Thereafter the productivity did not vary much from 1998-99 to 2002-2003.

But the productivity is declained to 2050 Kg/ha during 2003-04 compared to that in previous year. (Table 29) In Kerala application of HYV rice is not cent per cent.

Table 30
Productivity of local varieties of Rice in Kerala

Year	*Productivity (Kg/ha)*
1990-91	1833
1991-92	1833
1992-93	1919
1993-94	1884
1994-95	1894
1995-96	1842
1996-97	1933
1997-98	1866
1998-99	1894
1999-00	1929
2000-01	1854
2001-02	1965
2002-03	1701

Source: Directorate of Economics and Statistics.

Table 30 shows the productivity of local variety of rice was much lower than that of the HYV rice. The productivity of local variety did not vary much between the year except during 2002-03, when there was slight decline compared to previous year (Table 32) To improve the production, the farmers have to select HYV rice than the traditional varieties.

Table 31
Area and Production of Local Variety rice

Year	*Area (Ha)*	*Production (MT)*
1990-91	396634	727201
1991-92	374991	706141
1992-93	362512	695666
1993-94	335414	632033
1994-95	328845	622838
1995-96	307274	566001
1996-97	277497	536413
1997-98	218443	407553
1998-99	175533	332441
1999-00	138784	267731
2000-01	120768	223912
2001-02	94296	185326
2002-03	59714	101559

Source: Directorate of Economics and Statistics.

Table 31 clearly reveals that there was sharp decline in the area under local variety of rice cultivated. It has drastically declined from 396634ha in 1990-91 to 59714 ha druing 2002-03. The produciton was declined proportionately, as expected on the other hand, though the area under cultivaiton of HYV of rice and the produciton did not vary much form 1990-91 to 1998-99.

There was fluctuations between years during this peirod. There was gradual increase in area and productivity of HYV of rice in Kerala form 1999-2000 and it touched its peak high during 2002-03. Agian, the area and production declined during 2003-04.

Table 32
Area and Production of HYV of rice in Kerala

Year (1)	*Area (ha)* (2)	*Production (M Tons)*
1990-91	162816	359372
1991-92	166336	354209
1992-93	175095	389212
1993-94	172418	371905
1994-95	17445	352227
1995-96	163876	387025
1996-97	153329	334948
1997-98	168679	357057
1998-99	177098	394302
1999-00	211411	502955
2000-01	226687	527416
2001-02	222088	518178
2002-03	250804	587300
2003-04	238546	489123

Source: Directorate of Economics and Statistics, Economic Review 2005.

Table 33
Area Coverage of HYV Rice Over Total Area

Year	*HYV area (ha)*	*Total area Under Rice cultivation(ha)*	*% of HYV over total area*
1985-86	163278	678281	24.07
1990-91	162816	559450	29.10
1995-96	163876	471150	34.78
2000-01	226687	347455	65.24
2001-02	222088	322368	68.89
2002-03	250804	310521	80.77
2003-04	238546	287340	83.02

Source: Directorate of Economics and Statistics, GOK.

Table 33 shows that there was only 163278 ha of land under HYV rice during the year 1985-86, but after a period 20 years ie 2003-04 the area of HYV rice has increased to 238546 ha of land and its percentage over total rice area under Cultivation was 83.02 per cent.

Table 34
Area, Production and Productivity of irrigated Lands in Kerala

Year	*Area (ha)*	*Production (MT)*	*Productivity (Kg/ha)*
1990-91	225063	451106	2004
1991-92	228916	473337	2068
1992-93	212576	439552	2068
1993-94	209430	427511	2041
1994-95	249885	523971	2097
1995-96	234409	521239	2224
1996-97	230087	487152	2117
1997-98	202143	421011	2083
1998-99	196927	435963	2214
1999-2000	208740	494460	2368
2000-01	208047	481279	2313
2001-02	183962	433288	2355
2002-03	181561	433748	2389

Source: Directorate Economics and Statistics, GOK.

Table 34 Shows the total area, Production and productivity of irrigated lands in Kerala. The area of irrigated land showed a decreasing trend as the total area of rice cultivation was decreasing year by year and the production is also showed a decreasing trend. But their was an increasing trend in productivity. During the year 1990-91 an area of 225063 ha of land where irrigated and the production was 451106 Million Tonnes. But in the year 2002-03 there was only 181561 ha land under irrigation and the production was only 433748 Million Tonnes. The productivity in the year 1990-91 was 2004 Kg/ha. But it was 2389 Kg/ha during the year 2002-03.

Table 35 shows the total area of un-irrigated land under rice cultivation, its production and productivity. The production and productivity of unirrigated land was much lower than that of irrigated land. The production as well as productivity of this un-irrigated land could have been increased by converting these land into irrigated land.

Table 35
Area Production and Productivity of Unirrigated Land in Kerala State

Year	*Area (ha)*	*Production (MT)*	*Productivity Kg/ha*
1990-91	334387	635452	1900
1991-92	312591	587033	1878
1992-93	325062	645326	1985
1993-94	298402	576427	1932
1994-95	253405	451094	1780
1995-96	237410	431787	1824
1996-97	200739	384209	1914
1997-98	184983	343599	1857
1998-99	155704	290780	1868
1999-00	140984	276226	1959
2000-01	139408	270049	1937
2001-02	132422	270216	2041
2002-03	128960	255111	1978

Table 36
Season-wise area, Production and Productivity of Rice in Kerala during 2003-2004

Season	*Area (ha)*	*Production (MT)*	*Productivity (Kg/ha)*
Virippu	102770	220132	2142
Mundakan	147384	266674	1809
Puncha	37186	83239	2238
All Seasons	287340 ha	570045 MT	1984 Kg/ha

Source: Directorate Economics and Statistics - Economic Review 2005.

ECOLOGICAL LOSS DUE TO PADDY FIELD CONVERSION

Conservation of biological resources in the modern sense is the part of development and conservation means "the management of human use of biosphere. So that it may yield greatest sustainable benefit to present generations while maintaining its potential to meet the needs and aspirations of future generations. Thus conservation is positive, embracing, preservation, maintenance, sustainable utilization, restoration and enhancement of natural environment". But instead of conservating our rich biological resources, current process of development is depleting many biological resources at such a rate that they are rendered essentially nonrenewable.

Ecosystem destruction is one of the major threats of bio diversity. Ecosystem is the productive origins of planet and it surround us as forests, grasslands, rivers, coastal and deep waters, islands, mountains, and various agro-ecosystems. The fact is, we are utterly dependent on eco systems to sustain us and ecosystem yield goods and services that we cannot do without. Ecosystem make the earth habitable purifying air and water, maintaining biodiversity, decomposing and recycling nutrients, and providing myriad other critical functions. Harvesting the bounty of eco systems roots our economies and provides us employment, particularly in low and middle income countries. Rice fields are such a kind of eco systems, which yield goods and services to mankind. But, due to high destructions of this eco system, rice, the like line crop is becoming highly valuerable in the state Kerala. Table 2.21 shows that with in a span of 50 years, this tiny state has lost more than 50 per cent of its rice cultivated area . Paddy fields are recklessly being converted for the cultivation of other profitable crops like rubber, coconut, banana, Arecanuts etc. Conversion of this land is also for mining clay for brick industry. As an ecosystem paddy fields are unique and provide support for living organisms associated with it. Paddy is a water-loving crop producing enormous tangible and intangible goods and services to the human beings.

Table 37
Common Flora in the Surroundings of Paddy Fields

Vernacular Name (Malayalam)	*Scientific name*
Muthil (Kudangal)	Centella asiatica
Cheera	Amaranthus viridis
Brahmi	Bacopa Morrieri
Ponnamkanni	Alternanthaera sessilis
Thaal	Colocasia spp
Churuli	
Kattu Kaduku (Kallurukki)	Scoparia duleis
Panachi thall	Cerupto cora
Thakara	Cassia tora
Veli ehembu	Colocasia spp
Puliyarila	Oxalis corniculatus
Mudunjaehappu	

Contd...

Vernacular Name (Malayalam)	*Scientific name*
Vayal koovalam	Monocharia vaginalis
Paalthodu	Colocasia Spp
Vampalachap	Marsilia
Muthil	
Muthanga	Cyperus halpan
Vernacular Name (Malayalam)	*Scientific name*
Muthanga	Cyperus iria
Kattumalli	Chenopodium ambrozoides
Anachuvadi	Elephantopus scaber
Muyal chevian	Emilia sonchifolia
Vayal Malli	Hypericum Japonicum
Thumba	Leucas aspera
Manganari	Limnophila conferta
Karimkoovalam	Monocharia hastaefolia
Kizharnelli-1	Phyllanthus niruri
Kizharnelli-2	Phyllanthus urinaria
Kurumthotti	Sida aeta
Adakkamaniyan-1	Sphaeranthus indicus
Adakkamaniyan-2	Sphaeranthus africanus
Vayalchulli	Hygrophila auriculata
Muthanga	Cyperus rotundus
Kayyonnyam	Eclipta alba
Palluvedanachedi	Spillanthus calva
Poovankurunnela	Vernonia cineria
Vayambu	Acorus calamus
Inchi pullu	Cymbopogon citrates
Thottavadi	Mimosa pudica
Appa	Ageratum conyzoides

Source: Field Survey.

Table 38
Other Plants Found in the Paddy Fields

Vayambu	Acorus calamus
Injonganam pullu	Fimbri stylis miliacea
Parpidaka pullu	Hedyolis auricularia
Mulipannichedi-1	Lud wigia octovalvis
Mulipannichedi-2	Ludwigia perennis
Gear pullu	Eriocanlon truncatum
Naikkarimpu	Sacharum Spontaneum
Karuka	Cynadon dactylon
Kilukilukki	Crotalaria retusa

Source: Field Survey.

Table 39
Small creatures, Fish and Birds found in the Paddy Ecosystem

Small creatures	*Fish*	*Birds*
Paranjandu	Kiechoollan	Waterhen, Moorhen
Karuthanjandu	Aaril	Pigeon
Veluthanjandu	Varaal	Dove
Njavunica	Paral	Stork
Noonchi	Kallummemooti	King fisher
Ama	Mushi	Flycatcher
Thavala	Kari	Skimmer
Chakkamullan	Kada	
Thodah	Owl	
Nettipottan	Wag tail	
Kavoori	Dharan	
Konehan	Hawk	
Chemballi	Stork	
Vala	Heron	
Mullan	Teal	

Source: Field Survey.

The availability of above plants, creatures, fish and birds are highly related with the existence of paddy fields. Conversion of paddy fields will result in the destruction of the above eco system. This will badly affect the populatioin and availability of medicinal plants. In addition some of the rare species will become extinct.

Employment Opportunities in Paddy Cultivation

Need of labourers in Paddy cultivation is much greater than banana, rubber or any other cash crops. When there is a shift from paddy to cash crops, agriculture workers especially women workers lose their work to a great extend. There is gender discrimination in the different activities of paddy cultivation. items are ther work is done by both male and female workers. Some activities like transplanting, weeding, threshing etc are done by female workers. When there is a shift from paddy cultivation to banana, rubber, etc, the female workers loose their job, as there is no work which is specifically reserved for the female workers. So those female workers who depend upon this rice eco system of employment will suffer a lot.

Table 40
Employment Opportunities in the Paddy Cultivation

Activity	*Male*	*Female*	*Both Male and Female*
Land Preparation			✓
Ploughing	✓		
Seed Selection	✓		
Sowing	✓		
Transplantation			✓
Water Control/irrigation			✓
Fertilizer application			✓
Weeding		✓	
Kateling/guarding			✓
Harvesting			✓
Bundling		✓	
Transporting			✓
Treshing			✓
Winnowing		✓	
Cleaning		✓	
Storing	✓		
Marketing	✓		

Source: Field Survey.

Table 41
Gross Cropped Area of Important Crops in Kerala

(in percentage)

Crops	*1965-66*	*1985-86*	*1995-96*	*2003-04*
Rice	32.1	25.5	16.4	12.01
Coconut	22.5	24.7	30.3	35.06
Tapioca	8.6	7.8	4.1	4.3
Rubber	5.9	10.8	14.5	18.41
Pepper	4.0	4.0	6.1	8.00
Cashew	3.4	5.0	3.6	3.42
Arccaunut	2.4	2.1	2.3	3.61
Banana	1.8	1.8	2.3	4.15
Tea	1.6	1.2	1.1	1.43
Cardamom	1.2	2.0	1.4	1.61
Coffee	0.9	2.3	2.7	3.2
Other crops	15.6	12.8	15.2	4.8
All crops	100	100	100	100
Total (in 000 hectors)	2051	2807	3052	2584.690

* Calculated figures in percentage.

Source: GOK Department of Economics and Statistics.

The 41 Table reveals that there was a sharp decline in Paddy Cultivation. On the other hand Coconut, rubber, banana etc showed a positive trend. This is due to the decrease in income from paddy cultivation. On the other hand the positive trend in Rubber is due to the high income from rubber Cultivation. The same is the reason in case of coconut, banana etc. In 1965-66 only 5.9 per cent of the total cropped area was under rubber cultivation but in the 2003-2004 rubber cultivation was 18.41 per cent of the total area under cultivation. This is because of the profit volume was very high for rubber cultivation. Between 1965-66 to 2003-04 there was a 3 fold increase in the area under cultivation of rubber. In 1965-66 the area under coconut cultivation was 22.5 per cent, whereas in 2003-2004 the area under coconut cultivation was 35.06 per cent. Pepper, cashew, banana, arccanut, other crops etc showed an increasing trend both in area under cultivation as well as production, and productivity. The commercialization of agriculture in Kerala lead in anticipated shift in the crop pattern where cash crops began to dominate food crops. The ratio between cash crop and food crop in 1973 was 30:70 which was changed in to 70:30 by the end of 1990's. Rice is the major food in the state and due to its non-profit nature, farmers began to shift towards other profitable crop in the state and converted their land for non-agricultural purpose or for other cash crops like rubber, coconut, banana, arccanut etc.

Table 42
Cost of Cultivation Per ha Across Districts 2003-04

Name of district	*Cost (Rs/ha)*
Trivandrum	13346
Kollam	16771
Alappuzha	18904
Kottayam	16654
Idukki	14559
Eranakulam	12848
Thrissur	18828
Malppuram	14323
Palaghat	18695
Kozhikkode	9917
Kannur	20477
Kasargod	16697

Source: Compiled from working papers on Agriculture in Kerala, CDS, Trivandrum.

The cost of production of rice per ha is given in Table 42. Kannur which ranks first in cost of production is followed by Alappuzha and Palaghat. The cost of cultivation in Kerala is very high when compared to other rice producing states in India.

Table 43
Wage Rate of Agricultural Labourers in Kerala

Year	*Men*	*Women*
1994-95	64	42
1995-96	77	51
1996-97	92	61
1997-98	104	69
1998-99	112	72
1999-00	119	79
2000-01	123	82
2001-02	127	89
2002-03	145	100
2003-04	149	102

Source: Directorate of Economics and Statistics GOK.

The wage rate shows an increasing trend. It is however not related to the selling price of rice. This is also one of the reasons for increasing cost of production. Wage rate of agricultural labourers in Kerala is very high when compared to other states in India. During 1970-71, the average labour charges in Kerala was Rs. 5.09 where as in 2003-2004 it was Rs. 125.50. This shows about 2500 per cent increase or 25 times increase in wage rates. But the price of paddy was increased only 523 per cent 1970-71 one labour could be paid by selling 5.41 Kg of paddy whereas in 2003-2004 one Labour can be paid by selling 22 Kg of paddy.

This Table 44 reveals the cost of production of rice/ha in some of the selected states of India. Kerala ranks first in cost of produciton of rice whereas U.P has the lowest cos tof produciton. In Kerala cost of produciton per quintal was Rs. 522/- whereas the average cost of produciton was only Rs. 268/- Punjab is the state which has highest productivity and Assam is the state which has the lowest productivity. In Kerala hired labour is about 90 per cent, is the highest when compared to other state sof India. West Bengal and U.P are the states which have the lowest hired labour.

Table 44
Cost of Production and Yield/ha of Rice in Selected States of India

State	*Rice Area*	*Total cost*	*Cost/Qtl*	*Yield/ha*	*Labour days*	*% Labour cost to total cost*
Kerala	1 ha	20224	522	38.78	148	90%
Karnataka	1 ha	7074	202	35.02	98	70%
Andra Pradesh	1 ha	11647	258	45.12	32	65%
Assam	1 ha	5079	237	21.47	87	22%
Madhya Pradesh	1 ha	5075	228	22.21	82	53%
Orissa	1 ha	5984	281	28.33	131	49%
Punjab	1 ha	8426	183	46.03	62	57%
West Bengal	1 ha	7965	281	28.33	132	49%
Haryana	1 ha	10124	265	38.21	101	58%
Uttar Pradesh	1 ha	5060	175	28.85	102	49%
All States	1 ha	7154	268	36.43	110	58%

Source: Ministry of Agriculture, Government of India.

Table 45
Wage Rate Vs. Price of Goods

Year	*Men*	*Women Kg*	*Matta Rice per*	*Rubber Kg*
1999-00	119 (100.00)	79 (100.00)	13.34 (100.00)	30.99 (100.00)
2000-01	123 (103.4)	82 (103.8)	12.20 (91.5)	30.36 (98.0)
2001-02	127 (106.7)	89 (112.7)	13.40 (100.4)	32.28 (104.2)
2002-03	145 (121.8)	100 (126.6)	13.81 (103.5)	39.19 (126.5)
2003-04	149 (125.2)	102 (129.1)	13.89 (104.1)	50.40 (162.6)

Source: Directorate Economics and Statistics, GOK, 2005.
(Figures in brackets donote percentages).

The Table 45 reveals that the price of matta rice per kg during 1999-2000 was Rs. 13.34 and in the year 2003-04 it was Rs. 13.89 shows for 4.1 per cent increase in price. But the labour cost of men increased about 25.2 per cent and women about 29.1 per cent. In the case of rubber the price increased about 62.6 per cent in the year 2003-04 when compared to the year 1999-2000. Increased labour cost is also one of the reasons for the increased cost of produciton of rice in Kerala.

In Kerala, the price of paddy per quintal in 1974-75 was Rs. 223 whereas after 30 years, ie. on 2004 the price of paddy per quintal was Rs.694. There was only 3 times increase in the price of paddy whereas average labour charge increased about 25 times within a period of 30 years. This is also one of the reasons for a declining trend in paddy cultivation as the cost of production increases and majority of rice farmers are running at a heavy loss.

Table 46
Price of Paddy/Quintal for the Last 30 Years in Kerala

Year	*Price/Quintal*	*Price/Kg*
1974-75	223.38	2.23
1979-80	137.01	1.37
1984-85	200.76	2.08
1989-90	290.47	2.90
1994-95	494.86	4.94
1995-00	684.43	6.84
2003-04	694.4	6.94

Source: Agricultural Statistics, GOK.

Tabe 47
Average Annual Growth Rate of Area and Production of Major Crops 1991-92 Thru 2002-2003 (Percentage)

Crop	*Area*	*Production*
Rice	-4.73	-3.62
Tapioca	-2.69	-1.12
Coconut	0.30	2.64
Rubber	1.23	5.71
Food crops	-1.01	–
Non-food crops	0.66	–

Source: Directorate of Economics and Statistics. GOK.

Table 47 shows the grwoth rate of some of the important crops form the year 1991-92 to 2002-03. The Rice area shows a negative trend of -4.73 per cent and production also shows a decline about -3.62 per cent. Coconut, rubber etc shows a positive trend in growth rate of both area and production. Tapioca is also another important tuber crop which showed a declining trend both in area and production.

Table 48
Cropping Pattern Projection in the Future Markov Chain Analysis (%share)

Crop	*1975*	*1990*	*1995*	*2000*	*2005*	*2010*	*2015*
Rice	32	19	18	16	15	13	12
Tapica	12	6	5	5	4	4	3
Coconut	27	33	31	31	32	32	32
Rubber	7	15	17	18	19	20	21
Other crops	22	27	29	30	30	31	32

Source: Directorate of Economics and Statistics, Government of Kerala.

The cropping pattern under Markov Chain analysis shows a steep decline of rice from 32 per cent to 12 per cent. But coconut, rubber and other corps showed a positive trend in area under cultivation.

The Table 49 shows the comparative profit statement of Rice Cultivation in one acre and banana cultivation. The profit from rice cultivation was only Rs. 2400 as compared Rs.46000 from banana cultivation. This is also one of the reasons for a shift in cropping pattern from rice to cash crops such as rubber, coconut, banana etc.

Table 49
Cost benefit analysis of Rice and Banana Cultivation in 2004

Area (1Acre)	*Total Cost*	*Income*		
	Rice	*Banana*	*Rice*	*Banana*
Seedling	660	2000		
Fertilizers and Pesticides	2125	11500		
Labour	9530	11500		
Other expenditure		10000		
Total Cost	12315	40000		
Return from harvest			14750	86000
Net income			2435	46000
Net income rounded as			2400	46000
* Lease amount for one year				

Source: Field Survey.

The net return from rice cultivation is much lower when compared to other crops such as rubber, coconut, banana etc. The cost benefit analysis of 1 acre each of rice and banana is presented in the Table 49. The net return from rice is only

Rs.2400 as against Rs.46000 from banana. This is also one of the reasons for the shift in crop pattern ie. from rice cultivation to other remunerative crops.

Table 50 shows the contribution of Agricultural income to state's revenue. In 1993-94 the contribution of Agricultural sector was 6256crores of rupees. But during 2003-2004 it was only 5165crores. There was a decrease of 1091crores within in a period of ten years. The percentage to states revenue was only 13 per cent which was four per cent less than 2002-03 financial year.

Table 50
Growth of Agricultural Income in Kerala (1993-94 prices)

Year	*Agriculture Income*	*Rate of Charge over previous year*	*Percentage contribution tostates income*
1993-94	6256	–	26.23
1994-95	6897	10.25	26.62
1995-96	6947	0.72	25.78
1996-97	7115	2.42	25.39
1997-98	6777	-4.75	23.67
1998-99	6900	1.81	22.52
1999-00	7017	1.70	21.45
2000-01	5448	-22.36	16.23
2001-02	5312	-2.50	15.39
2002-03	5380	1.28	14.53
2003-04	5165	-4.00	13.00

Source: Directorate of Economics and Statistics, GOK.

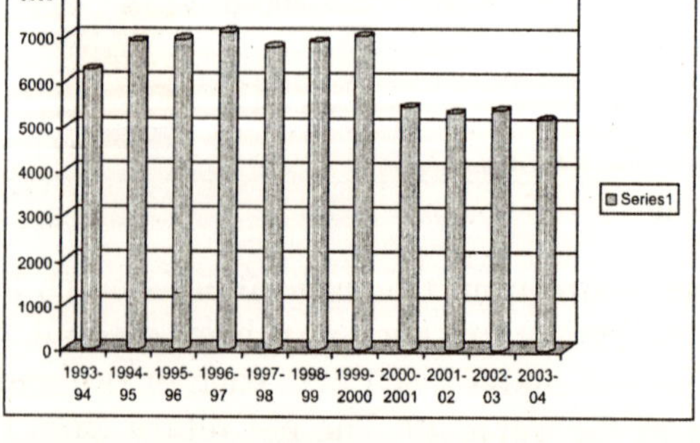

Figure 11 : **Growth of Agricultural income in Kerala (1993-94 prices)**

Table 51
Waste Land in Kerala (2002-03) in ha

District	*Waste land are (in ha)*
Thiruvananthapuram	6658
Kollam	8072
Alappuzha	1550
Pathanamthitta	7731
Kottayam	4880
Idukki	34813
Ernakulam	8454
Thrissur	7198
Palakkad	28356
Malappuram	12367
Wayanad	5184
Kozhikkode	2761
Kannur	6980
Kasargod	9814
Total	144818

Source: Land use Board & KSRSEC Economic Review 2003.

Table 51 revealed that waste lands in ha in different district of the state of Kerala. Iddukki showed the highest area of waste land followed by Palakkad, Malappuram, Ernakulam, and Kollamn Districts. Alappua District has the lowest area of waste land. The total waste land in Kerala showed about 144818 ha. The Govenrment of kerala through its agencies and with the help of other Non - Govenrment agencies should take urgent steps to cultivate rice in this waste land which were once the rice fields.

AREA AND PRODUCTION OF RICE IN ERNAKULAM DISTRICT

Ernakulam District is having a unique position in the matter of area under paddy cultivation and production. It occupies 4th position in the area of cultivation and also fourth place in production performance. More over the flourishing trade centres of rice and modern rice mills are located in this district. Out of the 120 modern rice mills using sophisticated production and processing techniques, 80 rice mills are operated in the revenue district of Ernakulam.

Table 52 showed the area and production of rice in Ernakulam District from 1991-92 to 2003-04. In 1991-92 there was 65001 ha of land under rice cultivation. Two to three crops were taken in a year from the paddy fields.

Table 52
Area Production of Rice in Ernakulam Districts

Year	*Area (ha)*	*Production (Tonnes)*
1991-92	65001	109484
1992-93	66158	113927
1993-94	61287	101346
1994-95	60018	101048
1995-96	56533	101951
1996-97	53988	93382
1997-98	46152	74234
1998-99	49730	84529
1999-00	42894	82326
2000-01	37433	65307
2001-02	32905	59723
2002-03	32072	60886
2003-04	29495	54044

Source: Directorate Economics and Statistics, GOK.

The production of rice was 109484 Tonnes during 1991-92 but during 2003-2004 it was only 54044 Tonnes.

The Table 53 showed the area, production and productivity HYV rice in Ernakulam District. During 1990-91 there was 19525 ha of land under HYV rice cultivated and production from the area was 35076. Due to the cultivatioin HYV rice the productivity of rice during 1990-91 was 1796 Kg/ha. During 2003-04 there was 26529 ha of land under HYV rice and production was 49662 Tonnes of rice. The productivity/ha was also increased by the use of HYV rice. It was 1872 Kg/ha during 2003-2004. Here also there is a decline trend both in area of rice cultivation as well as production. This is a common phenomenon everywhere in the state.

Table 53
Area, Production and Productivity of HYV Rice in Ernakulam District

Year	*Area (ha)*	*Production (Ton)*	*Productivity (Kg/ha)*
1990-91	19525	35076	1796
1991-92	21240	37058	1745
1992-93	21657	39908	1843
1993-94	23097	39422	1707
1994-95	19273	33448	1735
1995-96	18357	34174	1862
1996-97	15509	28415	1832
1997-98	31146	50695	1628
1998-99	41718	71204	1707
1999-00	37389	71130	1902
2000-01	33547	59502	1774
2001-02	28457	52421	1842
2002-03	28076	54403	1938
2003-04	26529	49662	1872

Source: Economic Review, 2005.

Table 54
Productivity of HYV of Rice in Ernakulam District

Year	*Productivity (Kg/ha)*
1990-91	1796
1991-92	1745
1992-93	1843
1993-94	1707
1994-95	1735
1995-96	1862
1996-97	1832
1997-98	1628
1998-99	1707
1999-00	1902
2000-01	1774
2001-02	1842
2002-03	1938
2003-04	1872

Source: Directorate of Economics and Statistics, GOK.

Table 54 indicated the area under local variety of rice as well as production. In 1990-91 there was 43553 ha of land under local varieties of rice cultivation and produced 67613 Tonnes of rice. The productivity of local variety rice during

1990-91 was 1552 Kg/ha. During 2003-2004 the local varities of rice were cultivated only 2966 ha of land and produced only 4382 Tonns. The productivity was only 1474 Kg/ha.

Table 55
Area, Production and Productivity Local Varieties of Rice in Ernakulam District

Year	*Area (in ha)*	*Production (Tons)*	*Productivity (Kg/ha)*
1990-91	43553	67613	1552
1991-92	43761	72426	1655
1992-93	44501	74019	1663
1993-94	38190	61924	1621
1994-95	40745	67600	1659
1995-96	38176	67777	1775
1996-97	38479	64967	1688
1997-98	15006	23539	1569
1998-99	8012	13325	1663
1999-00	5505	11196	2034
2000-01	3886	5805	1494
2001-02	4448	7302	1642
2002-03	3996	6483	1622
2003-04	2966	4382	1474

Source: Directorate of Economics and Statisttics, Government of Kerala.

FINDINGS

- Rice is a crop of tropics and subtropics, especially of the monsoon lands.
- 90 per cent of rice is grown in Asian countries.
- China is the largest producer of rice followed by India.
- 113 countries all over the world producing rice.
- India has the largest area under rice cultivation in the world.
- Only 43 per cent of the total area under rice cultivation is irrigated in India.
- West Bengal is the largest producer of rice in India.
- UP has the largest area under rice cultivation.
- In India rice is cultivated 23 per cent of the total land under various crops.

- Punjab ranks first in productivity.
- Andhra Pradesh ranks second in productivity of rice in India.
- In Kerala rice is cultivated under a diversity of climatic conditions, 3metres below Mean Sea Level (MSL) in Kuttanadu and 1400 meters as in High ranges (Munnar).
- In Kerala, Palakkad and Kuttanadu are known as rice bowls.
- Mid seventies were period of increased production and area of cultivation of rice in Kerala.
- Kerala is one of the states in India which has the lowest percentage of rice cultivation in India (0.76 per cent).
- Kerala witnessed a decline of 5 lakh Ha of land under rice cultivation over a period of two decades.
- During the year 2004-05, Kerala produced only 667105 metric tonnes of rice.
- In Kerala productivity shows an upward trend because of the use of HYV seeds.
- Kerala has 83 per cent coverage of HYV seeds of the total area under rice cultivation.
- The productivity of irrigated lands is higher than un-irrigated lands.
- Of the three seasons–'Mundakan, Virippu, Puncha', Mundakan shows the highest area under rice cultivation, but the productivity is higher in puncha seasons.
- During the year 1965-66 about 32.1 per cent of total area under rice cultivation in Kerala, but during the 2004-05 it was only 12.01 per cent.
- Remunerative crops like Coconut, Rubber, Banana etc. are increased their proportion of area under cultivation.
- In Kerala, of all the districts Kannur has the highest cost of cultivation.
- Of all the states in India, Kerala has the highest cost of cultivation of rice.

- Wage rate of agricultural labourers is the highest in Kerala than all other states in India.
- The wage rate of Agricultural labourers increased about 2500 per cent (25 Times) when compared to wage rates of 1970-71.
- The price of paddy per quintal is increased only 3 times when compared to prices of 1970-71.
- The cost of cultivation of rice per quintal is Rs. 522inKerala, which is the highest of all other states.
- The Kerala land Reforms Act 1970, insisted to keep a maximum holding of 5ha of paddy field per person and 10 ha to a family.
- The number of marginal farmers is highest in Kerala.
- The contribution of Agricultural income to the State's income in Kerala decreased to 13 per cent in the year 2003-04 from 26.23 per cent in the year 1993-94.
- Waste land in Kerala shows an upward trend.
- Of all the districts in Kerala, Idukki has the highest area of waste land.
- The area and production of rice is also decreased in Ernakulam district.

CONCLUSION

Rice is a crop of tropical regions; especially of the monsoon regions.90% of rice is grown in Asian countries. Almost all the countries (113) producing rice. Rice is the staple food of ½of the world's population. Major Rice producing countries of the world are the major consumers, so world trade is less than 5 per cent of total production of rice. China is the largest producer of rice in the world. India is the second largest producer of rice in the world. India has the largest area under rice cultivation in the world.

In India productivity of rice is comparatively less when compared to Japan, China, USA, etc. Japan has the highest productivity of rice in the world In India West Bengal is the largest produce of rice. Uttar Pradesh has the largest area under rice cultivation. The productivity of rice in India is very low. In India 23 per cent of the total land under rice cultivation. Andhra Pradesh ranking second in productivity of rice.

In Kerala rice is cultivated in a diversity of climatic conditions i.e. 3 meters below mean sea level in Kuttanadu and 1400 meters above the sea level in high ranges (Munnar).In Kerala area of cultivation as wellas production of rice is deteriorated every year. During 1965-66, about 32.1 per cent of the total area under rice cultivation. But during the year 2003-04 it was reduced to 12.01 per cent. This is due to the change in negative cropping pattern effect of cultivating remunerative cops like coconut, rubber, banana etc.During 1965-66 coconut was cultivated 22.5 per cent and rubber was cultivated only5.9 per cent but during the 2003-04 , the area under coconut and rubber were increased to 35.06 per cent and 18.41 per cent respectively.

The decline in area and production of rice is a serious threat to the food processing industry mainly the rice milling business in Kerala. There is a wide gap between the demand and supply of rice in Kerala. Now itself Kerala is depending very much on other states for food grains. The cluster of modern rice mills in Kalady and other modern rice mills in the state depend upon the states like Tamilnadu, Karnataka, Andhra Pradesh and even North Indian states for their raw material (paddy) requirements.

3

PADDY: RICE SYSTEM

Rice processing is as old as the cultivation of rice. Among agro-processing industries, rice processing industry is the biggest industry in India. India is the second largest producer of rice in the world, and also ranks first in the consumption of rice. So she has to convert large quantum of paddy in to rice before consumption. Thus rice processing industry is the largest agro-processing industry with 138000 units consisting 91280 hullers 4540shellers 8380 hullers cum shellers and 35080 modern rice mills in the country (2004). India process 128 million metric tonnes of paddy, it is not only mills rice but also it carries many other essential functions such as procurement, drying, storage and utilisation of by products. The rice system and its by products are clearly depicted in Figure 1.

The beginning of the technological aspects of rice-processing like milling, parboiling etc. were to be found in the traditional practices of India. The milling of paddy is as old as the cultivation of rice itself, and has been referred to even in the 'Vedas'. Different types of milling equipment for the shelling and polishing of rice for household use existed in Indian homes many centuries ago. The time from which parboiling came in to vogue is not known with certaininity, although the technical and the nutritional advantages of parboiling were known to our ancients. It is thought that parboiling came in to use mainly to facilitate the removal of husk from paddy and to minimise its breakage while milling.

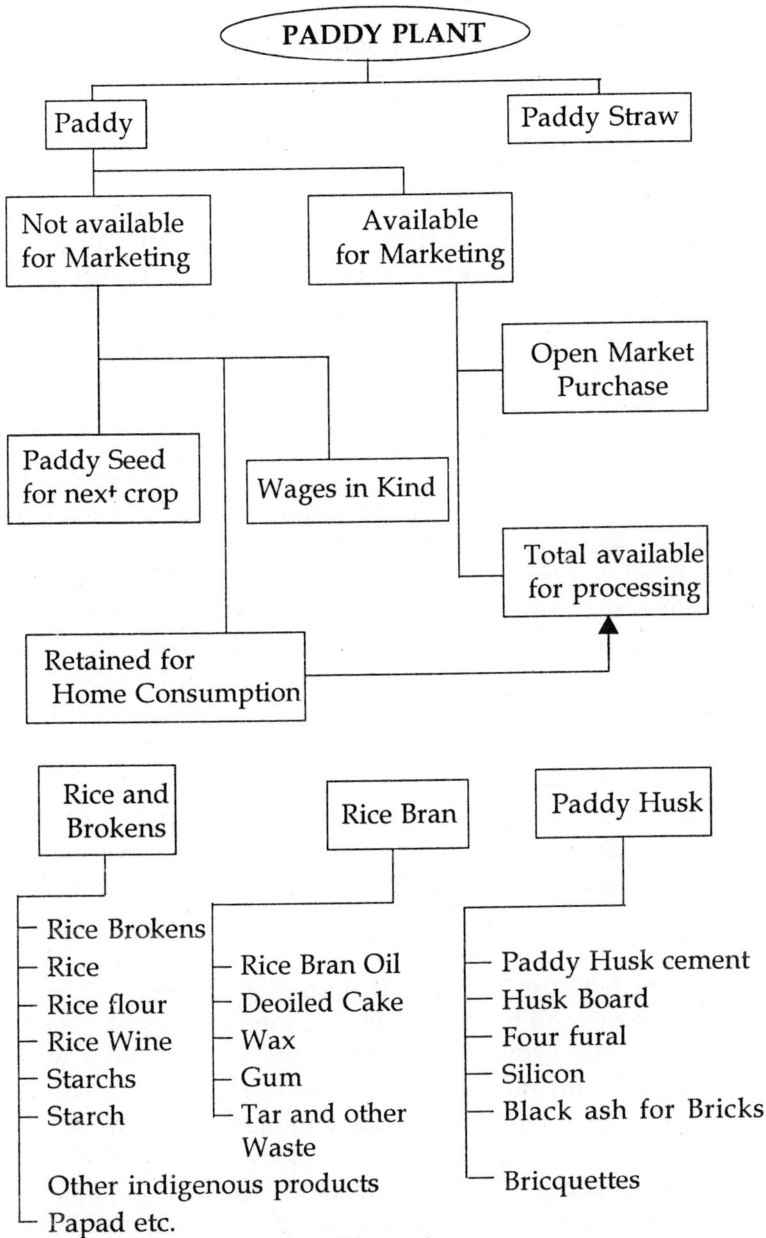
PADDY PLANT
Paddy
Paddy Straw
Not available for Marketing
Available for Marketing
Open Market Purchase
Paddy Seed for next crop
Wages in Kind
Total available for processing
Retained for Home Consumption
Rice and Brokens
Rice Bran
Paddy Husk
Rice Brokens
Rice
Rice flour
Rice Wine
Starchs
Starch
Other indigenous products
Papad etc.
Rice Bran Oil
Deoiled Cake
Wax
Gum
Tar and other Waste
Paddy Husk cement
Husk Board
Four fural
Silicon
Black ash for Bricks
Bricquettes

Figure 1

The major concern of milling paddy is to get maximum out-turn of better quality rice, with minimum broken and without damaging usable by- products. Whatever be the reason, the discovery of parboiling is one of the most important achievements in food science, and the credit of the discovery belongs to India. There is no record to show as to whom first discovered the process, but there is no doubt that parboiling was being practiced in India long before it was known to the other parts of the world. The practice spreads to different countries largely through the migration of Indians.

In the initial years, after independence hand pounding method of rice shelling was encouraged because of large employment potential in this method of converting paddy in to rice. The milling of rice in small quantities in the village homes using the various types of traditional equipment comes under the collective term "Hand Pounding". The chief virtue of hand pounding is that it gives medium polished rice with high 'thiamine' content. Due to certain disadvantages of hand pounding as compared with medicine milling, the breakage of grains in hand pounding is usually greater than in machine milling because of the abrasion in hand pounding, being less in machine milling. But during sixties when India faced food shortage, the need of modern rice mills was realized. The modernization includes scientific dripping, storage; parboiling and milling of paddy with rubber–roll – shellers. Consequently, the rice milling industry took a new turn and the Government of India decided to import machines and technology of seven modern rice mills. Modernization is much more capital intensive procedure, the government decided to provide credit and other facilities to the private millers as well, so as to encourage them to modernise their rice mills. There has been a tremendous growth in the number of rice mills with increasing production of paddy in the country.

During 1970, there were only 6 modern rice mills in our country and the total mills including these modern rice mills were only 59020. After a period of 35 years the number of modern rice mills are increased tremendously and the hullers and shellers remain almost stagnant. Now the government

Table 1
Rice Mills in India from 1970 to 2004-05

Year	*Hullers*	*Shellers*	*Hullers Cum shellers*	*Modern rice mills*	*Total mills*
1970	51880	2302	4832	6	59020
1975	80007	3676	7210	346	91239
1980	73306	4283	8065	5071	90725
1985	79197	4484	6654	17826	108161
1990	86007	4447	7859	29614	127927
1995	90091	4237	8362	33587	136247
2000	91287	4538	8385	35008	139298
2005	91800	4608	8398	35610	140416

*Provisional
Source: Ministry of Food Processing Industries, Government of India

encourages setting up of more rice processing mills in the private sector and also for the utilisation of by products such as rice bran, husk etc.

The Table 2 shows the state wise position of rice mills.West Bengal, Uttar Pradesh, Andhra Pradesh, Karnataka, Punjab etc. have the largest number of rice mills in the country. West Bengal is the state with the largest processing capacity in the country. About 119 lakh metric tonnes are processed annually. Andhra Pradesh occupies the first position with 12995 modern rice mills in the country with a processing capacity of 90 lakh metric tonnes, followed by Karnataka, with 3674 modern rice mills. The numbers of shellers were 1776 in Andhra Pradesh which shows the top position. It is observed that in those states where production is higher the number of rice mills is also higher in number. The number of modern rice mills has increased considerably over the time.

The numbers of modern rice mills increased from 6 during 1970 to 35610 in the country during 2004-05 (Table 1). There has been 5935 per cent increase in the total modern rice mills from 1970 to 2004-05. The 1970s to 80s were the decade when the maximum growth in all types of mills were observed, out of this Hullers are still constituting with 67.5 per cent of the total mills in the country.

Table 2
State wise Number of Rice Mills in India up to 2004- 05

States	*Hullers*	*Shellers*	*Hullers/ Shellers*	*Modern Rice mills*	*Total Mills*	*Production (in lakh tonnes)*
Andhara Pradesh	4609	1776	2364	12995	21774	90.14
Assam	431	14	2133	242	2820	33.90
Bihar	4749	63	9	51	4872	66.40
Gujarat	1890	159	67	1045	3161	8.27
Haryan	807	–	–	990	1797	18.47
Himachal Pradesh	890	1	3	222	1116	1.18
Karnataka	9131					
Madhya Pradesh	3918	201	262	1761	6142	58.39
Maharastra	8199	273	541	1759	10772	25.63
Orissa	6398	125	289	552	7364	62.26
Punjab	2815	---	---	1585	4400	69.43
Tripura	1030	6	8	1	1045	4.66
Uttar Pradesh	5707	562	150	1215	7634	103.63
West Bengal	9554	3	72	926	10555	118.97

Source: Ministry of Food Processing, Government of India.

PADDY PROCESSING

Prior to the actual milling operation, the paddy received from the farmer is cleaned in pre- cleaning machines. Foreign matter or impurities are removed to protect the processing equipment and improve the final product. The impurities can be divided in to large impurities, small impurities and impurities of the same size of the paddy grain. Large impurities normally consist rice straw, particles, loag strings, soil, and stones and sometimes iron parts. Small impurities consist of dust, sand, soil particles, weed seeds, insects and small stones. Impurities of the same size of the paddy grains can be empty grains, stones and iron particles.

Impurities in lighter weight than paddy can be removed by aspiration or by sieving. Large and small impurities heavier than paddy are removed by sieving; where as, particles of the same size but heavier than paddy can be removed by gravity separation. Foreign material about the same weight and size as the paddy grain is difficult to remove and it is disintegrated during the actual milling process. Weed seeds are generally small impurities normally separated through sieves. Iron parts or particles are removed by sieving, by gravity separation or by permanent or electro magnets.

MILLING PROCESS

Rice is obtained from paddy by milling, which removes the hull and bran. Paddy is a mixture of pericap, seed coat, and some of the aleurone layer.

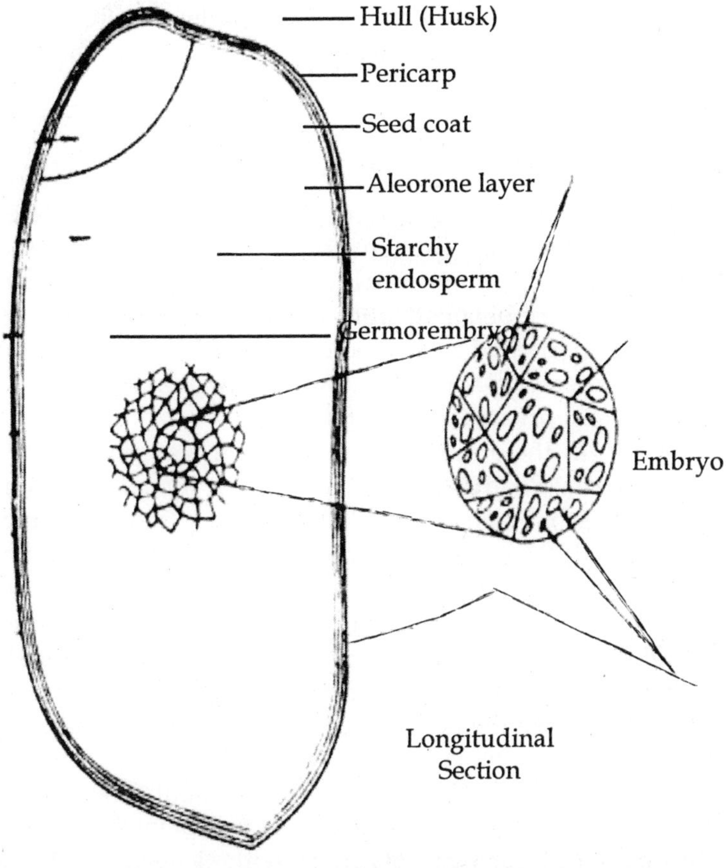

Figure 2 : **Diagramatic Representation of the Structure of a Paddy Grain**

The objective of milling is to get whole grain rice and preserve most of the rice kernels in their appropriate original shape. Some varieties of paddy do not yield much head rice (a rice kernel or a piece of kernel having length equal to or greater than ¾ of the average length of the unbroken kernel) because of their inherent poor milling quality or due to the effects of bad weather or un even processing conditions. Both pre- harvest and post- harvest factors cause breakage of rice during milling. Even if the proper precautions are used in post-harvest processing some varieties of paddy produce low head rice yield because inherent poor milling quality. To counter act this, pre milling treatments have been developed in India, Bangladesh, Pakistan, Burma, Srilanka, Malaysia, and Thailand.

PRE-MILLING TREATMENTS

Because the milling process has long been known to remove much of the vitamins and minerals from the grain, different types of pre-milling treatments of paddy have been devised to improve its milling, nutritional, cooking, and keeping quality. The rice obtained from milling pre treated paddy is known as parboiled rice; where as, the rice obtained from milling untreated paddy is known as raw rice or white rice. The different pre-milling treatments are;

Atapa: In the atapa treatment which was originated in Bengal, India. Paddy is soaked in water at room temperature for 24 hours and then dried in the sun (hence the name 'atapa' or sun dried). The dried paddy is then milled. During milling many of the grains will be in broken shape.

Balam: The treatment which was also developed in Bengal, is slightly better than 'atapa' because the paddy is sprinkled with hot water, which inflates the grain due to sudden thermal expansion, when the paddy is dried in the sun and milled the hull is easier to remove.

Josh: During the josh (boiling) treatment developed in 'Larkhana' in Pakistan, the paddy is first seined to remove the dirt. Large earthen pots filled with cleaned paddy and water are placed on a 15 cm layer of hull that is used as fuel.

The pots are then heated and remain on the fire all night. The next day the water is drained and the paddy is subject to a second heating in shallow iron pans placed on the fire for 1 hour. The paddy is then takes out of the pans and dried in the sun. Some times, soaking is done in iron tubes instead of in earthen pots. In this case, the water in the tubes is first heated to the boiling point and the fire is removed. The cleaned paddy is put in the tubes for 8 hours. The water is then drained and the paddy is heated in shallow iron pans and dried as described earlier. Because the rice is semi-cooked, the hull easily separates in milling and there is no breakage of grains. In addition, it is claimed that such rice has better keeping quality.

Sela: This treatment was originated and practiced in Saharanpur, India. In this method paddy is soaked in water at room temperature for about 24-48 hours and then gently roasted in hot sand (80-90 °c). Experience is required for judging the correct temperature of the sand and the duration of roasting. The heat supplied should be just sufficient to evaporate the moisture from the wet paddy with out causing porching of the rice. The roasted paddy is then further dried in the sand and milled.

Sidha: The sidha treatment was originated in Bengal. Paddy is soaked in water at room temperature for 24 hours, boiled for a few minutes, dried and milled. In this method, rice form over-soaked paddy becomes dark coloured; rice from over-boiled paddy becomes coase in appearance; and rice from over-dried paddy shows poor milling quality.

Parboiling: Parboiling of paddy is hydro thermal process that may be defined as the gelatinisation of starch with in the rice grain. Parboiling of paddy has been known to the orient for centuries. The parboiling process finds extensive application in the Eastern part of Southern India, Eastern Madhya Pradesh, and Uttar Pradesh. It is also well known in western Uttar Pradesh, Punjab, and Haryana in the form of sela process of parboiling. The process is also being used in Bangladesh, Pakistan, Burma, Srilanka, Malaysia, and Thailand. Parboiling has been practised in the United States,

Italy, U.K, on a commercial scale since 1940. Par boiling of paddy requires three steps; (1) soaking, (2) steaming, (3) drying.

In the soaking process the void spaces in the hull and rice kernel are filled with water and the starch granules absorb water and swell, which cause an increase in the volume of the paddy. During steaming soaked paddy is exposed to steam heat for a given duration and the starch present in the rice kernel is gelatinized. Subsequently the paddy is dried to 16 per cent moisture content, which imparts the hardness that the grains require for milling.

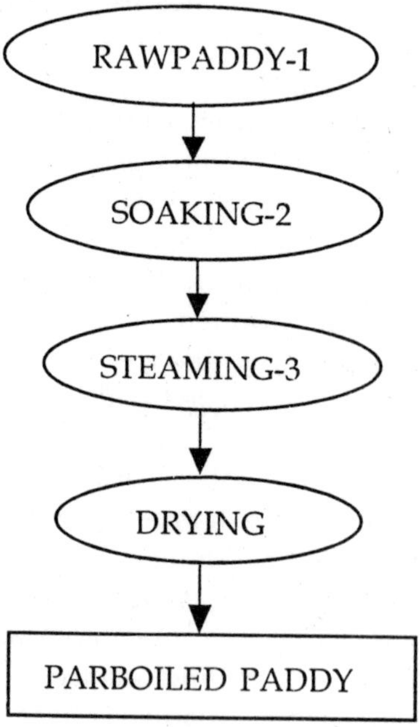

Figure 3 : **Steps for Parboiling Groups**

1. Traditional Methods; (a) Single Boiling (b) Double Boiling
2. Modern methods of par ``boiling; (a) CFTRI Method (b) Jadavapur university method (c) Converted process method (American) (d) Malek Process method (American) (e) Avorio process method (Italian) (f) Fernades process method (Surinam).

TRADITIONAL METHODS

Single Boiling Method

Paddy is soaked in ordinary water for 24-72 hours and then Transfer cylindrical iron kettle for steaming in small batches under atmospheric pressure. The parboiled paddy is then dried in the sun before milling.

Double Boiling Method

In this method, steam is injected in to the raw paddy in the steaming kettle before soaking. This hastens the soaking process. The hot paddy raises the temperature of the soak water to 45- 50°c, which reduces the soaking time to 24 hours. There after, soaked paddy is steamed as in the single boiling method.

MODERN METHODS

CFTRI Method

This is one of the modern method s of parboiling paddy practised in India, Pakistan and Srilanka. It was introduced by Central Food Technology Research Institute (CFTRI) Mysore in the mid 50 's. Large scale adoption of this method and production of parboiled paddy were started with the introduction of mechanical driers in modern rice mills.

Parboiling tanks are filled with clean water that is heated to temperature of about 85°c by passing steam through the coils inside the tank. Some times hot water is prepared in a separate hot water tank before it is pumped in to the parboiling tanks. The second process saves time and increases the capacity. The CFTRI method of parboiling has the following advantages over traditional method of parboiling.

1. There is reduction in soaking time to 4 hours which considerably reduces the processing time and increase production.
2. The bad smell is entirely eliminated.
3. Most of the micro organisms originally present will be destroyed because the paddy has been soaked in hot water and steamed.

4. The rice can be prepared on short notice depending up on the market demands.
5. The water requirement is smaller than the cold soaking method.

Jadavapur University Method

At Jadavapur University, studies were carried out to improve the method of parboiling by both batch and continuous techniques. The various operations of the integrated process include mechanical method s for soaking, steaming, cooling and drying. These studies resulted in a reduction in the time required for soaking to 2.5-3 hour depending upon the age and size of the grain. The two steps for soaking and steaming are done in the same vessel. The steaming time is reduced to 3-5 minutes. The short time of soaking and the elevated temperature eliminate the possibility of fermentation during and, there fore, reduce the chance of development of any off-flavour in the rice product. In this method the process is continuous and the rice product is lighter in colour because the steamed paddy is cooled before drying.

Converted Process Method

This process which was originated in 1941-42, was the first American par boiling process. The product is obtained by a complete gelatinization of the entire kernel. The parboiled product has an amber colour, is completely vitreous through out, and has no white starchy centre.

Soaking is an autoclave begins with de airation of the paddy by vacuum.This facilitates saturation and softening of the grain in water. A pressure treatment is applied to the soaking water in the auto clave that in combination with the vaccum reduces the soaking time to less than 3 hours.

Malek Process Method

This method was perfected a little later than the converted process. The amber coloured parboiled paddy is prepared by successive unit operation that leaves the grain remarkably hard. The paddy is steeped in tank filled with hot water for

3-6 hours. It is then cooked by the injection of the paddy. At the centre cf the rotary cylinder and extending along their length is perforated tube.

This tube carries hot water for steeping in the first cylinder, steam for cooking in the second and hot air for drying in the third cylinder.

Besides the above methods, there are different methods are also in practice, they are.

Brine Solution Method (Indian)

This is modified CFTRI method. The modifications and other development were done at the research development laboratory of the modern rice mill at Tiruvarur, in the latter part of 1969. The main advantage of this method is a reduction in the drying time resulting from reduction in the moisture content of the parboiled paddy.

Pressure Parboiling Method

This method was developed at Tiruvarur in the latter half of 1969. The principle of this method is the penetration of moisture in to the paddy in the form of water vapour under pressure which causes gelatinization of the kernel. The paddy is soaked for nearly 40 minutes at a Temperature of 85-90°c and then steamed under pressure for 18 minutes. The air entrapped inside the rice kernel is driven out by the penetration of water vapour, there fore the presence of white bellies in the resultant rice is avoided.It is claimed that the whole parboiling operation is completed in 1-1½ hours. The rice obtained in this method has a pleasing, slightly yellowish uniform col our and is having a great demand.

RPEC Method

(Rice Processing Engineering Centre, IIT, Kharagpur). Parboiling of paddy is a process of gelatinization of rice starch in situation which requires moisture and heat. Moisture and heat can be supplied to the paddy by soaking it in water that is at or a little above the gelatinization temperature of the starch, instead of supplying moisture and heat in two different operations, namely soaking and steaming as is presently done in conventional and modern methods of parboiling.

Sodium Chromate Method

The process consist of soaking paddy in a 0.05%sodium chromate solution for 40-48 hours. This control put re fractive for 3 days. The other operations ie. Teaming and drying are done in the usual way and no extra costs are involved. There is absolutely no smell in the soaked paddy, resultant rice or bran. Using this method, it is claimed that a saving in the cost of operation.

VALUE ADDED PRODUCTS FROM RICE

Nutrient status of rice is high. Due to its non-allergenic properties, this is the first cereal recommended for infants. Though rice is mainly consumed as whole cooked grain either in the form of raw- rice or modified rice. A variety of products for consumption as break fast food, snacks and beverages are prepared from it.

RICE PRODUCTS

Rice is consumed in many other ways than in the form of parboiled rice. They are;

Expanded Rice

It is prepared by heat expansion of milled paraboiled rice taking advantage of the property of cooked starch to expand when heated where by the product retains the shape of milled rice. Expanded rice is used in many forms as break fast dishes or snacks.

Puffed Rice

Puffed rice or porched paddy is produced by puffing of raw-paddy. When the uncooked endosperm material is suddenly exploded through the husk cover under the pressure of steam, and the product is very similar in appearance and properties to popcorn. Paddy can be put puffed by introducing it into an electrically heated rotator roaster adjusted to 275°c and allowed to puff until the missing sound stopped (40-45 seconds). Unpuffed grains and husks can then be separated. The starch content tightness of glumes enveloping the grains and differences in processing conditions has an influence on the puffing quality of the paddy.

Rice Flakes

Produced from milled rice by a process similar to that used for corn It is flattered or beaten parboiled rice of a thickness about0.6mm. The indigenous process consist in sand rotating (at 220-240°c) of soaked paddy followed by immediate flattering either by hand pounding with pestle or in edge- runner type machine. In western countries flaked rice is flaking.

Rice Noodles

A high quality rice noodle or vermicelli is prepared from lose milled rice or broken by wet milling or steeped rice, filtration or draining of the flour in cheese cloth bags, mixing 80°c water for 20 minutes and cooling of the cake, moulding in to balls of suitable size, surface gelatinizing by cooking in boiling water or steaming, kneading, extrusion through treatment of extruded noodles for surface gelatinization, soaking in cold water and drying in racks. Sheeted or flat noodles are prepared in Thailand from rice grits (dry-milled) and wet milled rice flour suspension, steam tunnel for gelatinization and then to dryer. The Japanese process for preparing flat noodles consists of washing milled rice, draining of the water in steaming mixer. The kneaded dough is pressed in rolling machine in to sheets of 1-3 mm thick, in a rolling machine, cut with a noodle cutter and packaged.

Flat Unleavened Rice Bread

(Similar to Indian chapathi or roti) is prepared in Pakistan. Rice cakes and rice pudding are favourite delicious of Japan. Rice cake is usually prepared from waxy milled rice by washing, steaming at 100°c for about 15 minutes to a steaming at to a moisture content of 46% grinding, packing in plastic film, pasteurizing in 80°c water for 20 minutes and cooling.Japan rice cake known as 'mochi' is usually cut into pieces, toasted and seasoned with soy sauce and eaten as snack.

FERMNTED PRODUCTS

Idli

Milled rice (mainly parboiled) and de-corticated black gram are separately soaked in water and wet-milled separately to coarse rice flour and smooth gelatinous black gram paste. These are mixed with 0.8% salt and the thick batter is fermented at room temperature, steamed and served hot.

Dosai

This is practically the same as idli but usually contains less black grain. The thin batter after fragmentation is fried in flat iron pan.

Appam

Raw–rice forms the sole ingredient of appam mixed with coconut water and is undergoing a slight fermentation.

Puttu

Powdered rice steam cooked in coconut shell or bamboo tube, traditionally prepared. For preparing the 'puttu', the rice powder need not be fermented.

Beverages

Rice based beverages are in use in many countries. Philippines rice wine (Taphy), rice vinegar, rice beer, rice murcha of Nepal, and 'sake' of Japan and some of the alcoholic beverages produced from rice. An alcoholic beverage 'shonti annam' is produced in certain parts of Andhra Pradesh from rice brokens.

MEDICINAL USES OF RICE

In India, especially in Kerala with its hoary traditions in the Ayurvedic system of medicine and any practising physicians, rice and rice products continue to be used in medicine. The wild rice (vari) belongs preumabily to the 'Sali' group and 'Navara' under the sub group 'sashlikam'. The varieties of rice broadly grouped as 'Sali' and 'vreehi'–in addition to 'Navara' two other varieties are also specially mentioned as medicinally important viz. 'Dhadhukani' and 'Raktha Sali' (Pigmented vari). 'Navara' is the variety exclusively utilised in what is called 'The Pancha Karma' treatment involving baths and massages for treatment in paralytic conditions. Roots of wild rice and 'Navara' find use in decease of kidney and bladder.

Rice poultice is said to be an excellent application for abscesses, boils, ulcers and other local inflammations. Rice flour or powder dusted thickly over the surface has a cooling and smoothing effect in prickly heat and other inflammatory conditions of skin. It finds application in cases of burns, scalds as well. 'Kanji vellam' (water de-canted after cooking) as such is a good drink in gastric ulcer and with a lemon juice or salt, is used as demulcent and refrigent in fever as also in inflammatory conditions of stomach, bowels and kidneys. Gruel made from beaten rice (Avil) is considered to be a good cooking drink in dysentery and diarrhoea.

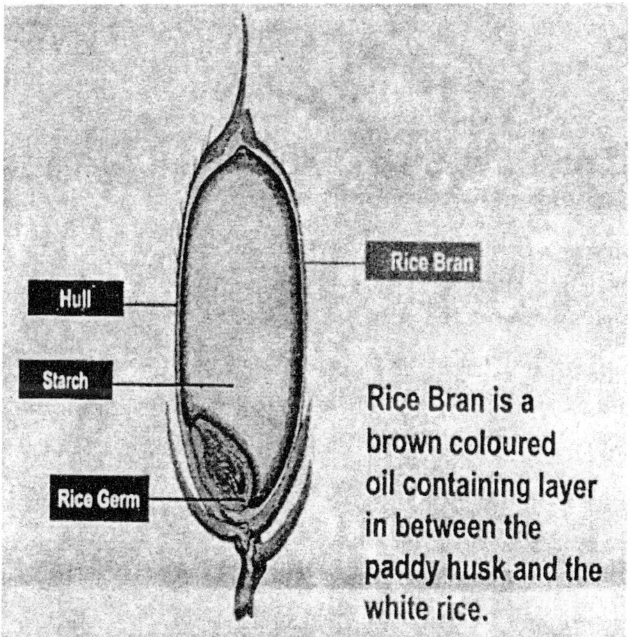

Figure 4

RICE BRAN OIL

Rice bran, the out layer of brown rice is the most valuable by product of rice milling industry. Generally rice bran consists of pericap, aleurone layer, germ and part of endosperm. Bran removal amounts to 4 to 9 per cent of the weight of paddy milled. True bran amounts to 4 to 5 per cent only; rest is polish consisting of inner bran layers and portion of the starchy endosperm. Rice bran contains vitamins, minerals and many other useful ingredients. Bran is a potential source of vegetable oil. Because of its nutritional value, it is being utilised as feed for poultry and live stock. More stable defatted bran contains high per cent age of protein, vitamins and minerals than fully fatted bran is an excellent ingredient for both food and feed, Crude bran oil of high FFA (Free Fatty Acids) is used for the manufacture of soap and fatty acids.

Edible grade oil is produced by refining crude bran oil of low FFA content (about 5%) in addition tocoferrol waxes of high melting point suitable for various industrial purpose are the by products of the bran oil industry.

Processing of rice bran for separating oil was prevalent in China, Japan and Korea for centuries ago. This rice bran oil industry is started in India very recently. Two important processing methods employed were batch production by hydraulic presses and continuous production by the use of expellers. Before pressing the bran is purified steam cooked, dried, pre processed to remove the oil. The amount oil left in the residue was about 6to 12per cent and 4 to 8 per cent under by hydraulic pressing and expeller conditions respectively. High FFA (Free Fatty Acid) oil is obtained from rice bran. The rice bran oil is further processed to obtain edible oil.

The Country's production of rice bran is around 82 lakh tonnes, with a potential to produce over 9 lakh tonnes rice bran oil per annum. Currently the industry is processing about 32 lakh tonnes of rice bran producing over 4.80 lakh tonnes per annum of rice bran oil of which 3 lakh toees are edible grade. This is mainly used in the manufacture of vanaspathi and a small quantity of 50,000 tonnes is being refined, packed and sold.

Table 3
Production of Rice Bran Oil during 1994-95,95-96,97-98.

	1994-95	*1995-96*	*1996-97*	*1997-98*
Paddy production (MT)	121.7	119.4	120.8	122.3
Rice Production (MT)	81.8	79.6	81.2	82.5
Total Rice Bran Potential (LT) (7.5%of Rice)	61.0	60.0	61.0	61.9
Rice Bran Oil Potential (LT) (15% of recovery)	9.1	9.0	9.1	9.3
Actual Rice Bran Processing(LT)	31.7	32.0	32.0	33
Actual Production Rice Bran Oil (LT)	4.5	4.8	4.8	5.0
Untapped Potential Rice Bran Oil (LT)	4.5	4.2	4.3	4.3

Table 3 explains that during 1994-95, India Produced only 4.5LT of rice bran oil with a potential to produce 9LT and an untapped potential of 4.5LT of rice bran oil. During 1995-96, India produced only 4.8 LT of rice bran oil and an untapped potential of 4.2 LT of rice bran oil. In the year 1996-97 also India produced only 4.8 LT of rice bran oil and an unused potential of 4.3 LT of rice bran oil. In the year 1997-98 India produced 5 LT of rice bran oil and with an untapped potential of 4.3LT of rice bran oil.

Solvent Extractors Association of India(S E A) says the country is facing a shortage of edible oils and to bridge the gap, it is forced to import a million tonnes of vegetable oil per annum, at the cost of foreign exchange. Rice bran is perhaps the best source of edible oils available in the country.

Table 3 shows the extraction capacity and capacity utilization of oil extracting units in the country. The table explains an average capacity utilisation of 34.5 per cent only and an untapped capacity of 65.5 per cent.

The edible oil industry in India as a whole is not working satisfactorily. Their capacity utilization is 33 per cent only. The use of imported oil in vanaspathi is on increase, 14.2 per cent in 1995-96, 38.8 per cent in 1997-98, and 42.4 per cent in 1998-99.

India with a paddy production of 80 milliontonnes in the year 1983 produced only a meager quantity of 5000 tonnes

Table 4
Capacity Utilization and Production of Oil Extracting Units (2003-04)

Category	*No. Of Units*	*Annual Capacity (MT)*	*Capacity utilisation*
Oil Mills (Crushing Units)	15,000	36.00	40%
Solvent Extraction Plants	600	31.00	33%
Vegetable Oil Refineries	400	5.00	32%
Vanaspathi (HydrogeneratorUnits)	204	3.3	33%

Source: Solvent Extractors Association (SEA).

edible grade rice bran oil, Where as Japan with 15.3 Million Tonnes of paddy in that year produced 600,000 tonnes of edible grade rice bran oil though India more than 100 solvent extraction plants as early as in 1970, it produced 21000 tonnes of rice bran oil alone that too industrial grade.

Table 5
Rice Bran Processed and the Production of Rice Bran Oil in India (Metric Tonnes)

Year	*Rice Bran produced*	*Rice Bran Edible Oil*	*Rice Bran oil Industrial use*	*Total*
1970–71	170,000	–	21,000	21,000
1971–72	220,000	–	30,000	30,000
1972–73	185,000	–	25,000	25,000
1973–74	165,000	–	24,000	24,000
1974–75	160,000	–	23,000	23,000
1975-76	265,000	–	36,000	36,000
1976-77	540,000	–	70,000	70,000
1977-78	566,000		80,000	80,000
1978-79	680,000	2500	98,500	1,01,000
1979-80	786,500	2450	1,10,400	1,12,850
1980-81	922,000	4,000	1,26,000	1,30,000
1981-82	10,60,000	10,000	1,40,000	1,50,000
1982-83	10,90,000	26,500	1,26,000	1,52,000
1983-84	13,00,000	23,000	1,60,000	1,83,000
1984-85	14,10,000	19,200	1,81,000	2,00,200
1985-86	14,7,2700	32,850	1,85,050	2,17,900
1986-87	17,28,400	93,350	1,59,000	2,52,350
1987-88	19,40,500	1,18,650	1,59,400	2,78,050
1988-89	20,92,250	1,24,650	1,75,500	3,00,150
1989-90	23,40,400	1,41,125	2,08,600	3,49,725
1990-91	25,35,000	1,62,750	2,06,800	3,69,550
1991-92	25,53,400	1,97,700	1,68,750	3,66,450

Contd...

Year	*Rice Bran produced*	*Rice Bran Edible Oil*	*Rice Bran oil Industrial use*	*Total*
1992-93	27,53,404	2,06,527	1,84,612	3,91,139
1993-94	27,88,318	2,30,917	1,76,539	4,67,456
1994-95	27,50,677	2,45,883	1,53,420	3,99,303
1995-96	29,73,588	2,59,938	1,68,402	4,28,340
1996-97	28,79,302	2,65,689	1,55,456	4,21,125
1997-98	28,47,412	2,84,073	1,36,892	4,20,965
1998-99	29,44,683	3,02,054	1,25,219	4,27,273

There after, the extraction of rice bran had slowly picked up, and by 1978-79 98500tonnes of industrial and 2500 tonnes of edible grade rice bran oil where produced. The number of solvent extraction industry stepped up the production of the above oils. For the Indian solvent extraction industry the year 1991-92 was a turning point: only from this year the production of edible grade rice bran oil (168750 tonnes). Thereupon much emphasis was given for producing edible grade oil. By 1998-99 India produced 302054 tonnes of edible grade and 125219 tonnes of industrial grade rice bran oil from 2944683 tonnes of rice bran.

Rice bran oil is a better cooking medium nutritionally than kardi oil, but due to lack of awareness among consumers, demand is not picking up, demand is not picking up this has further affected processing and production of rice bran oil. Rice bran oil as the ideal oil for margarine and shortening. Rice bran oil containing vitamins antioxidants and other nutrients. It is highly rich in vitamin E complex, toeopherols and tocotrienl, and unique antioxidant known as gamma aryzanol, high quantities of phytosterols, poly phenols and sqnalene. It has a very good shelf life compared to other cooking oils. Rice bran oil is extremely light, versatile and delicious to fry or sautein salad dressing, baking dipping oils etc. Rice bran oil has the best balance of sautrated mon- un saturated and poly-unsaturator fats as recommended by such organizations, as the American health association and World Health Organization.

The Rice mill cluster in and around Kalady has a total production capacity of 300 metric tonnes of rice bran per day, annual production of about 90000metric tonnes. This rice bran can used to extract rice bran oil. Before 2004, there was not a single unit in Kerala to extract rice bran oil. Earlier this rice bran was sold to middlemen for processing in the adjoining states like, Karnataka, Tamilnadu etc. In order to utilize the rice bran, KRMC (KaladyRice Miller Consortium) established a major plant at Kalady to tap the un utilized rice bran. So that they will get the maximum price for their by products. They have established a Common Facility Centre Expeller unit and producing rice bran oil in the common brand name called "LEADS".

RICE MILLING IN KERALA

Rice is the staple food of Keralites' from time immemorial. It has been an essential ingredient of a 'Malaya lees' diet, especially for the old and middle aged generation. Even the new generation in Kerala and abroad promote; Malaya lee' food mainly made of rice and its different forms. Paddy is the main crop in Kerala and rice milled from paddy.

Earlier paddy processing was considered as a house hold business. Employing traditional method of hand pounding such as (a) 'Dhenki' (b) hand stone* ('chakku')* (c) 'Ural and Ulakka' (d) 'Mortar and Pestle'

Paddy processing was done by the female members of the family. As time passed, with the increase in production and productivity as well as the change of joint- family system to nuclear family system, rice mills on modern l on behalf to flourish. With the introduction of high-yielding variety of crops which in turn resulted in a massive increase in productivity led to the emergence of middle men in paddy trading. Bulk purchases were made by them on behalf of the traders and products were flown from production centres to the trading centres this in turn necessitated the establish ment of sophisticated modern rice mills.

In Kerala rice milling was a traditional business. Decades back each family has their own paddy field and produced sufficient paddy for their requirement.

* Versa Cular (Malayalam)

They used single boiling system or double boiling system with the use of a utensil called 'chembu' (a large utensil made of copper) and dried in the sunlight and milled it in traditional equipment called 'Ural, Ulakka' mechanism. Slowly the system changed. The growth of rice mill industry can be traced to several distinctive phases.

Phase-1 : (pre-1955); prior to 1955, paddy was boiled in small quantity in small pots or utensils and dried in sun light. The dried paddy was de- husked by means of 'Ural Ulakka mechanism' or hand pounding.

Phase-2 : (1955 to 1970); After 1955 mortarised hullers has been used for milling paddy. They used mild steel vessels for parboiling and dried in yards under sunlight.

Phase-3 : (1970-1990); Since 1970 commercial type small rice mills started in Kerala with an average production capacity of 3-4 metric tonnes per day. They parboiled paddy in mild steel boxes and dried in yards under sunlight. They milled this paddy in motorised hullers. These conventional type mills could not make quality rice as they did not have adequate paddy cleaning, parboiling, drying and milling facility. More over these mills remain closed during seasons of rainfall as they were depending on drying yards and sunlight for drying. Their out put were not polished, and includes parts of mud, stone, husk, bran and other foreign elements.

Phase-4 : (post 1990); Since 1990 modernisation and mechanisation of parboiling and drying system of paddy emerged. Modern automatic rice mills produce superior quality rice with the introduction of parboiling, steam drying and modern milling system. Rice is free of mud, stone, husk, bran etc. After 1990's many conventional units underwent modernisation.

1990's witnessed the change of Kerala society that rice became a consumer item available in the nook and corner of the state, packed and branded in different brand names such as 'Pavizham,' ' Nallari', 'Ponnari,' 'Sadhya', 'Swad', 'Keerthi', 'Horse', 'Mayil mark', 'Ruchi' ' Annam' 'Maveli', 'Periyar' 'Kerala' etc.

While analysing the factors that led to the modernisation of rice mills were due to;

1. Most of the rice mills (traditional) were having a capacity of 2 tonnes per hour or less. It is to be noted that bigger capacity of rice, the more economical it is in terms of operating cost.
2. The equipments used in the mills were old and outdated technology leading to process losses, lower yields and higher power consumption.
3. Human errors were reduced as the modern rice mills are using Hi-tech systems.
4. Production at large scale as the total plant usage time is increased.
5. Modern rice mill technology helps to monitor paddy input to rice output ratio in a higher level.
6. Labour cost and maintenance cost is the minimum.

All the above factors contributed much for the modernisation of rice mills and in Kalady as per the information collected through field survey.

Raw Paddy Inspection

The raw paddy stored in the godown is inspected and fed to raw paddy receiving tank.

Raw Paddy Cleaning Section

It consists of raw paddy receiving tanks, raw paddy elevators, and paddy cleaner cum de-stoner and double elevator. Paddy may contain up to 5% of wastages such as lumps of soil, stones, stalk and chaffs. Raw paddy from the receiving tank is fed to paddy cleaner cum de-stoner by raw paddy elevator, which removes lumps of soil, stones, stalk, and chaffs. The cleaned paddy is then supplied to the storage tank of parboiling unit by double elevator.

Parboiling Section

Parboiling is one of the critical process which determine the quality and taste of parboiled rice. Even though, we are using the superior quality paddy, the precise control of the temperature pressure, time and water requirement of par boiling is required for getting the superior par boiled rice.

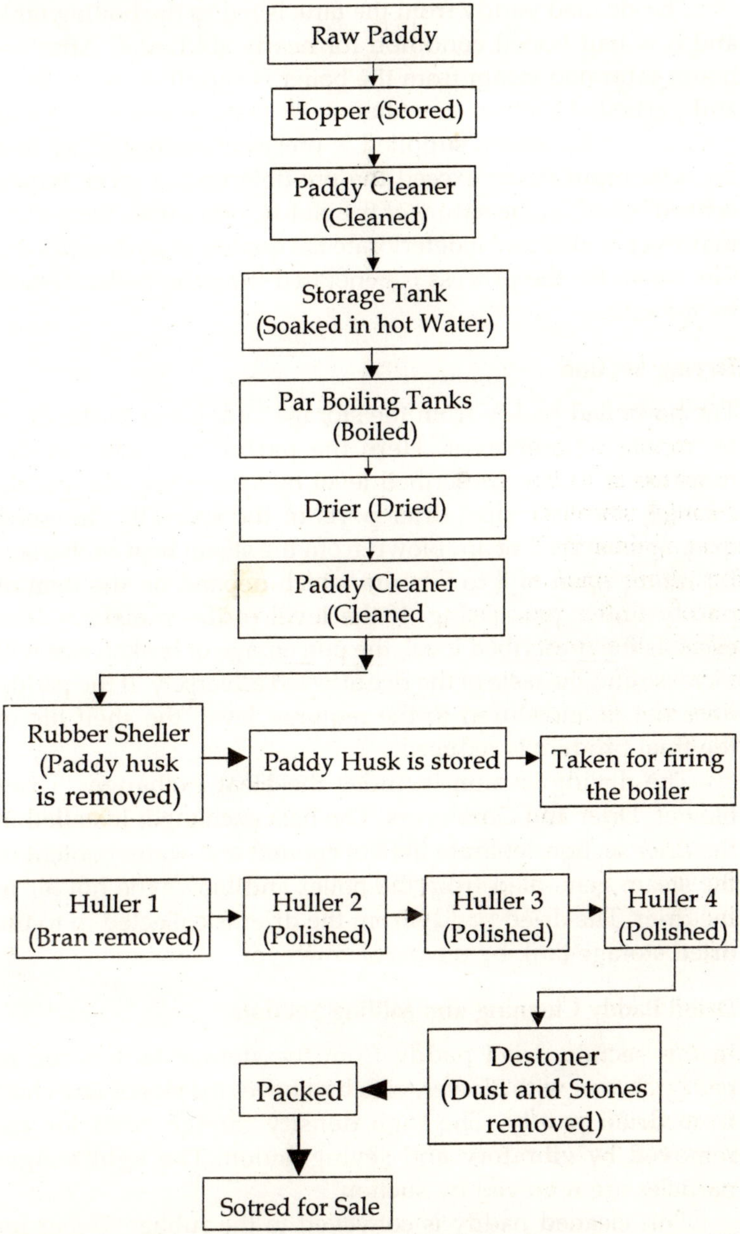

Figure 5: **Flow Chart of Production Process**

The cleaned paddy from the tank is fed to the boiling tank and it is half boiled condition for nearly six hours. After six hours saturated steam from the boiler is supplied to this tank and parboiled with in three hours. Here the temperature and pressure of the steam supplied is precisely controlled so that the heat input never exceed the pre-determined level, which is fixed based on the nature of the paddy, other wise the paddy may over-boiled and it deteriorate the quality of parboiled rice. The steam for the process is generated from the boiler owned by the unit.

Drying Section

The parboiled paddy from the storage tank is fed to the drier by means of conveyor. Here the parboiled paddy is de-moisture in to the prescribed level by spring ling the paddy through stainless steel drier ports of the specially designed drier against the hot air, blown from the steam heat exchanger for a time span of 8 to 9 hours which depend on the item of paddy under processing. If the level of de- moisterisation exceeds the prescribed level, the percentage of broken rice will increase and the taste of the rice affected adversely. If the paddy does not de-moistured to the required level, the shelf life of the final product is reduced.

The drying section includes the Heat exchanger, Drier blower, Drier and Conveyors. The heat exchanger installed in the drier section separate the hot content and water content of the steam generated from the boiler and blows the hot air to the drier. The dried paddy from the drier is collected in to the dried storage tank by means of conveyor.

Dried Paddy Cleaning and Milling Section

In this section dried paddy from the storage tank is fed to paddy cleaner with blower, which removes the stones and chaff from dried paddy. The high density foreign particles are removed by vibratory and seving action. The light weight particles are removed by suction.

This cleaned paddy is conveyed to the rubber Sheller for de-husking by vertical elevators.The husk is removed between two rubber rollers with out affecting the shape of the rice. By using this rubber sheller, it can minimize the percentage of the broken rice produced during the process. Also it can adjust the percentage of the rice bran with rice as per the requirement of the customer. About 5% to 20% paddies remain un-husked. The mixture is conveyed to variable stroke paddy separator where husk is sucked out by husk aspirator. Rice grains are collected and fed to the elevator for whitening and polishing. 5% of the 20% of the paddy is also get separated and discharged at a third point and is send back to the rubber sheller for further de-husking.

Half portion of the de-husked rice is conveyed to huller-1 and remaining portion is conveyed to huller-2, where the outer layer of bran is removed by rollers. The bran is sieved and separated.

This rice is again supplied to huller-3 and 4th for further polishing. Here iron rollers polish the rice and sieves and blades remove wastages. This polishing will give an elegant appearance to the rice.

The polished rice from the Huller is fed to de-stoner which removes the foreign particles such as stones, metal particles etc. It also separates the broken rice and collected separately.

The rice bran collected by bran shifter contains proteins and vitamins and extensively used for edible oil extraction and cattle feed production. The husk is collected in a tank and used as a fuel for boiler.

Colour Sorting Section

The polished rice from milling section is fed to imported electronic colour sorter for removing dis-coloured kernels; Peck defects and foreign material from rice. It is also capable of a simultaneous colour and chalky rice sot. The sorted rice is stored in a storage tank.

Finished Goods Inspection

The rice from the storing section is inspected and assured the quality.

Packing Section

The sorted parboiled rice are weighed and then packed and stitched in 10 kgs, 25kgs, 75 kgs, and 100kgs in jute bags.

The quantity and quality of processed rice and its conversion cost and the use of by-products are of vital importance for the economy of Kerala. The need for the increased production, consiquently high market arrivals of paddy in Kerala, the techniques used have changed from hand pounding to the integrated rice mills having the facility for most economical use of all the by- products like straw for paper, bran for edible oil and cattle feed, husk for fur fural and briquettes and rice for human consumption

Table 6
Rice Processing Statistics

Various products	*Percentage*
Rice	65
Husk	22
Bran	6
Broken Rice	4
Waste	3
Total	100

Source: Rice mill owners Association.

Table 6 explains the rice processing statistics,only 65 per cent of paddy realized as bold rice and 22 per cent processed as husk are used as fuel for boiling plant. Bran realised only 6 per cent which can be further used for rice bran oil extraction and the remaining bran after extraction can be used for cattle feed. Broken rice and waste can also be used as cattle feed.

As stated earlier, paddy production is highly concentrated in the districts of Palakkad and Alappuzha. These two areas are known as the 'rice bowls of Kerala. About 50 per cent of paddy for rice processing is supplied by these two districts alone. It was observed that the number of rice shellers was 399 in 1975-76 in Alappuzha and 378 in Palakkad district alone. Ernakulam which ranks 3rd in area of cultivation and 4th in production of rice has 403 rice mills of which 8 of them were modern rice mills in the year 1975-76. The total installed capacity was 483 tonnes per day. The total number of rice mills increased to 1503 during 1985-86 of which modern rice mills increased to 18. During the year 1999 -2000 the number of rice mills stood at 1400 of which 53 of them were modern rice mills. Obviously the installed capacity also increased from 483 tonnes per day to 1000 tonnes representing two fold increase in processing. 1990s witnessed the change of rice trading from the districts of Palaghat and Alappuzha to Ernakulam because of the concentration of modern rice mills in the banks of river Periyar which is the perennial source of water for rice processing.

Table 7

Number of Working Rice Mills from 1975- 2004 in Kerala

Year	*Shellers*	*Hullers*	*Modern rice mills*	*Total No. of rice mills*
1975-76	480	380	–	860
1980-81	550	600	–	1050
1985-86	350	500	10	960
1990-91	150	150	50	350
1995-96	120	80	60	260
2000-01	100	38	110	248
2004-05	80	20	120	220

Source: Kerala Rice Mill Owners Association.

Now in Kerala 120 Modern rice mills are operating which produces about 6 lakh metric tonnes of processed rice for consumption. The average investment of a modern rice mill is estimated to be around 1.5-2 crores of rupees. According to the Kerala Rice Mill Owners Association, the only organisation working in this sector stated that the average turnover from this sector alone were more than Rs. 2000 crores on an average.

Table 8 shows the district wise position of modern rice mills in the state of Kerala. In Thiruvananthapuram district only 2 modern rice mills are working. This is because of the proximity to the Nanchinadu district of Tamilnadu where the rice production is in a large scale especially in the Kanyakumari area where the main cultivation is paddy. There are large numbers of rice mills operating and processing rice, this rice is consumed mainly in Thiruvanathapuram district, where the paddy production is also in decreasing level. Another feature

Table 8
District Wise Number of Modern Rice Mills in Kerala, 2004-05

Name of district	*No. of modern rice mills*
Thiruvananthapuram	2
Kollam	–
Pathanamthitta	–
Alappuzha	4
Kotayam	2
Idukki	1
Ernakulam	80
Thrissur	8
Palaghat	20
Malappuram	–
Kozhikkode	–
Wayanad	2
Kannoore	1
Kasargod	–
Total	120

Source: Kerala Rice Mill Owners Association.

is that the rice mills are highly concentrated in Ernakulam district where rice is processed by the use of paddy from different parts of the country. In Ernakulam district alone there are more than 80 modern rice mills operating and processing nearly6lakh metric tonnes of rice on an average. Even though Palaghat ranks first in area as well as production of paddy in the state, only 20 modern rice mills are operating there. There are districts where there are no modern rice mills. Kollam, Pathanamthitta, Malappuram, Kozhikkode and Kasargod districts have no modern rice mills at present. These districts are fully depending Ernakulam, Palaghat, Thrissur districts for rice and other rice products.

A modern rice mill gives direct employment around 10 people and another 30-50 people are working on contract basis. Modern rice mills on an average have a capacity to process 24 metric tonnes of rice in one shift. The average time required for one shift is 8 hours. One modern rice mill works two shifts per day on an average.

The raw material–paddy–required for this industry is mainly procured from other states. Only less than 15 per cent of the total requirement for paddy is supplied by the state. Quality of rice is decided mainly by the quality of paddy available and by the polable soft water available for paddy processing.600 liters of waste water is generated while processing 1 metric ton of paddy. So the availability of water resources is an important factor for the installation of modern rice mills. This is one of the main reasons for clustering of modern rice mills in Ernakulam district where water is available in plenty from the perennial source of river Periyar.

Table 9
Taluk Wise Distribution of Modern Rice Mills in Ernakulam District, 2004-05

Name of Taluk	*No. of modern rice mills*
Aluva	45
Kanayannoor	2
Kochi	1
Kunnathunadu	20
Kothamanglam	4
Muvattupuzha	5
Paravoor	3
Total	80

Source: Kerala Rice Mill Owners Association.

Table 9 Reveals the Taluk wise distribution of modern rice mills in Ernakulam district. Aluva taluk has the highest density of modern rice mills in the district of Ernakulam followed by Kunnathunadu Taluk. Both these taluks are situated with in the banks of river Periyar. In the Aluva taluk, Kalady, Manjapra, Thuravoor, Mookannoore, Malayattoor-Neeleswaram Grama Panchayath and Angamaly Municipality have the highest number of Modern rice mills. In Kunnathunadu taluk, Okkal, Koovappady, and Perumbavoor Municipality have the highest number of Modern rice mills. Fifty two Modern Rice Mills are operating in and around Kaldy.Out of this 52 units working in and around Kalady, 42 units are selected as sample units for applying the of Porters Diamond Model of cluster. The major findings and facts arrived at on the basis of field investigation, are summarised below.

- Parboiling of rice processing is practiced in India from ancient times.
- Modern rice Mills were started in 1970 in India.
- The number of Modern rice mills was increased from 6 in 1970 to 35610 in 2004.
- Rice Bran is the main by product of rice processing industry.
- Rice bran oil is a good cooking medium.
- Rice bran oil extraction units started in India very recently.
- Rice bran available in Kerala is not fully utilized.
- The KRMC (Kalady Rice Millers Consortium) is marketing their Product in the common brand name called "LEADS".
- The growth of rice milling in Kerala has four distinct phases.
- From the year 1980, the rice mill business in and around Kalady shows an upward trend.
- In Kerala 120 Modern rice Mills are functioning at present.
- The average turnover from rice mill business in Kerala estimated to Rs.2000 crores per year.
- Of all the districts in Kerala, Ernakulam ranks first in the number of Modern rice mills (80), followed by Palakkad (20).
- A modern rice mill gives direct employment to 10 persons and indirect employment to 50 on an average.
- Of all the taluk in Ernakulam district, Aluva taluk has the highest number of modern rice mills (45) followed by Kunnathunadu taluk (20).
- 52 modern rice mills are operating in and around Kalady.

CONCLUSION

Rice processing is as old as the cultivation of rice. India process about 128 million metric tonnes of paddy. Parboiling method of rice processing was practiced in India from ancient times. Different types of milling equipment for the shelling and polishing of rice for household use existed in Indian homes many centuries agó. The major concern of milling paddy is to get maximum out- turn of better quality rice, with minimum broken and with out damaging usable by- products. The discovery of parboiling is one of the most important achievements in food science, and the credit of the discovery belongs to India.

In India modern rice mills were started in the year 1970. The number of modern rice mills were increased from 6 to 35610 in the year 2004-05.WestBengal is the largest producer of rice and with the largest processing capacity. Among the by- products of rice mill business, rice bran is the main by-product. From the rice bran, rice bran oil can be extracted and it can be used either for industrial purposes or cooking purpose. Rice bran oil is a good cooking medium. But the rice bran oil extraction units are started in India very recently.

In Kerala, the modern rice mills were started during 1980's. At present, there are 120 modern rice mills are operating through out the state and producing about 6 lakh metric tonnes of processed rice. In Kerala, Palakkad and Kuttanadu in Alappuzha district are known as the 'rice bowls', but the modern rice mills are concentrated mainly in Ernakulam district. Out of the 120 modern rice mills in the state 80 modern rice mills are operating in Ernakulam district. Among the 7 taluks in Ernakulam district, Aluva taluk has the highest number of modern rice mills followed by Kunnathunadu taluk.In Aluva taluk alone 45 modern rice mills are operating.There is a cluster of modern rice mills in and around Kalady in Aluva taluk.From time immemorial Kalady was a trading centre for rice. The development of Kalady rice mill cluster was rapid after1980's. There are 52 modern rice mills are operating in and around Kalady.

A modern rice mill give direct employment on an average 10 persons and indirect employment to 50 persons. At present more than 4000 persons are employed by the rice mill cluster in and around Kalady. A modern rice mill has an average capacity of 24 metric tonnes of rice in one shift. The average time required for one shift is 8 hours. One modern rice mill works two shifts per day on an average.

4

CLUSTRING OF MODERN RICE MILLS IN KALADY

Kalady, the birth place ofAdvaitaPhilosopher and Saint Jagad Guru Adisankaracharya is one of the important pilgrim centers of Kerala. From the year 1980 onwards, Kalady has been emerged as a prime centre of Rice milling in Kerala. Majority of Modern rice mills in Kerala are located in Ernakulam District. There are 120 modern rice mills in Kerala as per records out of them 80 registered modern rice mills are in Ernakulam and 52 are located in and around Kalady, of which 30 are fully automated and 50 are semi automated. One fully automated unit is having the processing capacity of 100 tonnes per day, now working at an average capacity of 50 tonnes per day. The modern rice mills can work two shifts /day. Semi automated rice mills are having a capacity of 60 tonnes/day. Thus altogether the modern rice mills in Kalady have the processing capacity of more than 4000 tonnes /day, producing about 2800 tonnes of rice, 200 tonnes of rice bran- 1600 tonnes of paddy husk.

Due to the conglomeration of modern rice mills in Kalady, this area has been developing at an amazing pace and as a brisk trading centre of rice in the state. This chapter deals with the identification and analysis of the cultural and historic and socio-economic reasons behind the clustering of modern rice mills in Kalady on lines with Porter's Model of clutstering were used for milling rice. In order to overcome the foodgrain shortage, Government of India imported 6 modern rice mills from Germany to different parts of the country other than the state of Kerala . During this period hullers were established in different parts of the state for milling rice. Even at this stage riceprocessors at the household level was going on inspite of the emergence of such small ricemills with minimum level of processing facilitities. Cultivators of paddy with the help of brokers began to sell their paddy on a large scale and the same was purchased by millers and stored in the mill premises itself. They began to employ men and women at the various stages of processing such as soaking, steaming, drying, and milling. At this stage there was no Branded rice, every smallscale millers produce rice in the common form and sold to wholesalers and retailers. Marketing of rice from Kalady to different parts of the state without the help of advertisements. This period onwards the Government of India started `National Seeds Corporation' and began to distribute yielding variety seed to cultivators. The mill owners began to form their own trade unions such as Rice Mill Owners Association.

EMERGENCE OF SOPHISTICATED (HI-TECH) MODERN RICE MILLS

1990's witnessed a remarkable change in the processing and marketing of 'Kalady Rice'. The high demand for kalady rice from all parts of the state has necessitated the traders and processors to bring paddy in large quantities. They began to collect paddy from outside kerala such as Tamilnadu, Karnataka, Maharastra,UP, Andhra Pradesh etc.At this stage the rice processors also needed plants and machineries having large processing capacitities, even 100 tonnes/ day which lead to the estsblishment of modern rice mills with automatic processing techniquws to meet the ever increasing need for high quality rice. Due to the introduction of highly sophisticated modern rice mills some of the existing traditional mills were converted into modern rice mill and in the struggle for modernization some of the non- modernized mills were closed down. A new class of commission agents consisting of paddy brokers, lorry brokers, rice bran brokers emerged due to the large scale production of rice.

Another important mile stone in the history of rice mills in Kalady is due to cut-throat competition between the modern rice mills. They began to market their products in brand names. They began to practice modern marketing technique to increase the market share of each brand. The conversion of traditional mills in to modern ricemills necessitated huge amount as capital investment. An amount not less than 1.5 crores of rupees are required for the establishment of a modern rice mill. This in turn led to the high involvement of commercial banks and other financial institutions like KFC, IDBI, and ICICI etc. The un - skilled workers engaged in the traditional mills were thrown out of employment as the labour requirement is very low for modern rice mills. Due to the continuous inflow of trucks lorries and other national permit vehicles which carries paddy from states like Tamilnadu, Karnataka, UP,Punjab, and Maharastra the outflow of natural resources available in and around kalady such as river sand crusher metal, granite, latrite, plywood, furniture, spices, etc. and finished products helped Kalady develop as a brisk trading centre.

There are 52 modern rice mills operating in and around Kalady. The clustering of rice mills in Kalady and the help of several ancillary units such as Rice Bran Oil Extraction units, jute bag manufacturing units, Engineering workshops, Rubber Sheller manufacturing units,Weighing bridges, offered direct and indirect employment to hundreds of people who where thrown out of employment from traditional rice processing units. These units are utilising the by- products of modern rice mills. There are large number of people who are working as paddy brokers, rice bran brokers, truck and lorry brokers, rice traders etc.

This chapter makes an in depth analysis of the overall performance of modern rice mills in Kalady.

One of the important advantages of clustering of industries is the concentration of small and medium firms on place bound regional concentration. The high linkage net working and joint action reduced transaction cost and there by resulted in collective efficiency of the cluster. The following are the features of clustering of modern rice mill in and around kalady.

1. Geographical proximity of modern rice mills
2. Dominance of small and medium sized units
3. Close inter firm collaboration
4. Iner-firm competition based on innovation

The rice mill clustering in Kalady is going to improve like;

1. Brass parts and components cluster–Jamnagar,Gujarat
2. Diesel engine cluster, Rajkot,Gujarat
3. Brass ware cluster, Moradabad,UP
4. Sports goods cluster,Meerut,UP
5. Cottonkite wear cluster of Tiripur, Tamilnadu
6. Hi- Tech industrial net work in Banglore,Karnataka
7. Agra foot wear cluster
8. Kottayam leather industries
9. Perumbavoor ply wood industries
10. Kannur handloom and garment s clustering

The focus of study is the development of Kalady Modern Rice mill clustering. A detailed study is made regarding economic process, inner dependence etc. of the Rice mill clustering in and around Kalady

SELECTION OF SAMPLE UNITS

The list of modern rice mills in and around Kalady supplied by Kerala Rice Mill Owners Association, Kalady Rice Millers Consortium, Small Scale Industries Department and District Industries Centre,Ernakulam, Government of Kerala, are the main source for selection of sample units. According to them there are 120 units in Kerala out of which 80 are located in Ernakulam district alone. There are disricts where there is no unit of modern rice mill. Out of this 80 units 52 are located in and around Kalady. Out of these 52 units only 42 units operated and supplied information for this study.

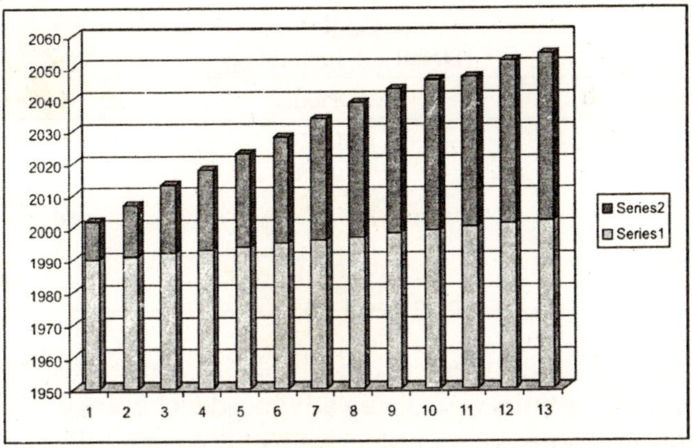

Figure 1: **Profile of the Modern Rice Mills in Kalady**

Table 1

Number of Modern Rice Mills in and Around Kalady

Year	*1990*	*1991*	*1992*	*1993*	*1994*	*1995*	*1996*	*1997*	*1998*	*1999*	*2000*	*2001*	*2002*
Rice mills	12	16	21	25	29	33	38	42	45	47	47	51	52

The growth of Kalady rice mill cluster was rapid after 1980 in terms of the number of units manufacturing ' matta rice' branded as 'Kalady rice'. Till the late 70's there was no modern rice mills in the country. But after 1970 the government itself started 6 modern rice mills for which the machinery and equipments were imported from Germany. In Kerala, modern rice mills were established from 1980 onwards.

Table 1a

Distribution of Units According to Nature of Work Under Taken

Activity nature	*Number of units*	*Percentage to total number*
Parboiled rice	42	100
White rice	8	19

All units(42) reported that they are mainly concentrated in producing parboiled rice. Only very limited units produce white rice (8units).

Table 2
Details of Technology

Technology used	*No. of units*	*Percentage*
Highly Advanced	15	36
Advanced	6	14
Moderate	21	50
Average	–	–
Backward	–	–
Total	42	100

Only 15 units were using highly advanced technology (36 per cent). 6units were using advanced technology. Majority of units (21) were using moderate technology (50 Per cent).

Table 3
Details of Automation

Nature of plant	*No of units*	*Percentage*
Fully automated	15	36
Semi-automated	27	64
Non-automated	–	–
Total	42	100

Table 3 classifies modern rice mills in and around Kalady as fully automated, semi-automated, and non- automated. Of the total 42 units under study reported that only 15units were fully automated, 28 units (64 per cent) were semi-auto mated.There was not a single unit operated as non- automated. This means that there was not a single unit working on traditional lines.

Table 4
Classification of Units on the Basis of Age

Age of units	*No. of units*	*Percentage*
Below 3 years	–	–
2-5 years	8	19
5-10 years	20	48
10-15	12	29
15-2020 and above	2	4
Total	42	100

Source: Field Survey.

There are 20 units (48per cent)established in between 5-10 years and 12 units in between 10-15 years old (29 per cent) only 2 units are in between 15-20 years. These units were the pioneer's of modern rice mills in Kalady, after that 50 more rice mills came into existence and now it is known as Kalady cluster of modern rice mills.

Table 5
Nature of Acquisition of Units

Nature of acquisition	*Proprietary*	*Partnership*	*Private Ltd. Co.*	*Total no. of Percentage*
Starting new units	5	20	5	30 (71%)
Purchased old units	2	5	1	8 (19%)
Inherited	1	3	-	4 (10%)
Total	8	28	6	42 (100%)

Source: Field Survey.

Out of the total 42 units under study, 30 units were newly started (71 per cent),8 units were purchased and converted to modern mills(19 per cent).Only 4 units were in herited(10per cent). Of the total 42 units 8proprietary, 5 were newly started, 2 were purchased as existing units and 1 unit was inherited property. Of the total 28 partner ship units 20 were newly started, 5units were purchased and 3units were inherited. Only 6 units were running on private limited company out of which 5 were newly started and 1 unit was purchased from existing mill.

Table 6
Nature Ownership of the Sample Units

Type of ownership	*No. of units*	*Percentage to total no.*
A. proprietary	8	19
B . Partnership	28	67
C. PrivateLtd. company	6	14
D. Public Ltd.co.	–	–
E., Co-operative units	–	–
Total	42	100

Source: Field Survey.

Major share of modern rice mills in and around Kalady were operating in partnership basis. Out of the total 42 units where from information was collected about 28 units were running on partnership basis, (67per cent) 8 units were running on proprietary basis (19 per cent) and the remaining units were operating as private limited companies (14 per cent).It is to be noted that there is no government owned as well as co-operative rice mill units in and around Kalady.

Table 7
Classification on the Basis of Capacity Utilization

Capacity utilization	*No. of units*	*Percentage to total units*
Units having 50 per cent capacity utilization	8	19
50-75 per cent utilization	33	79
75-100per cent utilization	1	2
Total	42	100

Source: Field Survey.

On the basis of capacity utilization 33 rice mills were working on 50-75 per cent, representing 79 per cent of the total units, 8 units were working up to 50 per cent capacity utilization, representing 19 per cent of the surveyed units and only 1 unit which was working on 75-100 per cent capacity scale which was only 2 per cent of the total units.

Table 8
Classification of Modern Rice Mills on the Basis of Processing Capacity Per day

Capacity of processing	*No of units*	*Percentage to total units*
Less than 50tonnes per day	15	36
50-60 tones per day	17	40
60-70tonnes per day	4	10
70-100 tones per day	3	7
100 tones per day	3	7
Total	42	100

Source: Field survey.

Of the 42 units, 15 units reported that their processing capacity was less than 50 tones per day, representing 36 per cent of the total unts. There were 17 units more than 50-60 per cent capacity level representing 40 per cent of the total units. Only 3 units are working at 100tonnes per day representing 7 per cent of the total units surveyed.

PROFILE OF THE ENTREPRENEURS

Table 9 gives the major high lights of the entrepreneurial characteristic of the sample units. The educational profile of the owners of modern rice mills under study is given separately for each segment.

T
able 9
Educational Qualification of Entrepreneurs (Responded 120 Entrepreneurs)

Educational qualification	*Percentage to total number*
Illiterate	--
Primary education	55
Secondary education	23
Technical training	4
Graduation	15
Post Graduation	3
Total	100

Source: Field survey.

As about the educational profile of the entrepreneurs out of 120 persons who were the owners of modern rice mills in Kalady interviewed and they revealed that only 66 persons(55 per cent) got primary education, 28 persons (23 per cent) got secondary education, only 5 persons (4 per cent) technically trained, 18 persons (15 per cent) were graduate in different disciplines and 3 persons acquired post graduation and higher qualification such asM.B.A etc.

Table 10
Age Profile of Owners of Rice Mill (Only 120 Persons Responded)

Age	*No. of Owners*	*Percentage to total Number*
Up to 20	--	--
20 to 30	--	--
30 to 40	20	17
Age	*No. of Owners*	*Percentage to total Number*
40 to 50	78	64
50 and above	22	18
Total	120	100

Source: Field survey.

The age pro file of the entrepreneurs shows that the majority of them belongs to the age group of 40 -50 years (78persons) followed by 50 and above group (22 persons). There were 20 people who belongs to the younger age group of 30-40 category (17 per cent).

Table 11
Place of Origin of Entrepreneurs

Place of Origin	*No of units*	*Percentage to total*
Local Area	40	96
Out side the local area but Inside the district	2	4
Out side the District and inside the State	--	--
Out side the state	--	--
Total	--	--

Source: Field survey.

Of the 42 units surveyed as sample units enquiry regarding the native place and origin of the owners of modern rice mills proved that 96 per cent of the owners belongs to Kalady and surrounding places. Only 4 per cent belongs to out side Kalady but inside the district. No person belong to out side the district and out side the state.

Table 12
Nature of Ownership of the Premises of Modern Rice Mills

Nature of owner ship	*No. of units*	*Percentage to total no.*
Own premises	39	93
Rented premises	3	7
Total	42	100

Source: Field survey.

Majority of rice mills in Kalady owns its own premises(39units) and 3units are functioning in rented buildings. The same premises was used for storing paddy (raw material).

From the table it was observed that 52 per cent of the rice mills surveyed had mobilized fixed capital from the scheduled commercial banks, 14 per cent from private banks and 29 per cent from other financial institutions such as KFC, SIDBI etc.

Table 13
Source of Fixed Capital

Source of fixed capital	*No. of units*	*Percentage to total units*
From private banks	6	14
From schedule banks	22	52
From friends and relatives	--	--
From other financial institutions	12	29
From local money lenders	--	--
From family source	2	5
Total	42	100

Source: Field survey.

Table 14
Distribution of Modern Rice Mills According to Source of Working Capital

Sources of working capital	*No .of units*	*Percentage to total*
Bank credit	28	67
Suppliers credit	-	-
Own savings	8	19
Other sources	6	14
Total	42	100

Source : Field survey.

From the Table 13 it was reported that 28 units borrowed from banks (67per cent)and 8 units had collected working capital from their own savings (19 per cent). Only 6 units collected its working capital from other sources.

Table 15
Distribution of Rice Mills According to Investment in Plant and Machinery

Investment in lakhs	*No. of units*	*Percentage to total no of units*
25-30 lakhs	4	10
30- 40 lakhs	23	55
50 lakhs and above	15	35
Total	42	100

Of the 42 units surveyed 10 per cent of units had 25–30 lakh investment in plant and machinery, 55 per cent units had investment in between 30-40 lakhs and 35 per cent units have investment in plant and machinery above 50 lakh.

Table 16
Source of Capital for Expansion by Modern Rice Mills

Sources of expansion	*No. of units*	*Percentage to total*
Profit re invested	1	2
Loan from banks	32	76
Loans from relatives and friends	-	-
Personal savings	2	5
Other institutions	7	17
Total	42	100

Source: Field survey.

76 per cent of the owners of the surveyed units revealed that the investment for capital expansion by rice mills from loans advances from banks only 1 unit (2 per cent) re-invested their profit, 2 units from their personal savings and 7 units (17 per cent) collected capital for expansion purpose from other source.

EMPLOYEMENT PROFILE

Table 17 gives the employment profile of the modern rice mills in and around kalady. It is to be noted that the role of skilled workers is a must for running each unit. In every unit there is an employment of minimum of 5 workers to a maximum of 60 workers. These workers can be classified in to (a) skilled workers (b) unskilled workers (c) office staff (administrative staff).

Table 17
Classification of Rice Mills on the Basis Number of Workers Employed

No. of workers	*No. of units*	*Percentage to total no*
Up to 25	16	38
Between 25-40	10	24
40-50	8	19
50-60	5	11
60 and above	3	8
Total	42	100

Source: Field survey.

As per Table 17 revealed that there were 16 units which employed workers up to 25 (38 per cent of the units), 10 unit employed more than 25 workers (24 per cent), 8 units employed more than 40 workers (19 per cent) 5 units employed more than 50 workers (11 per cent) and 3 units employed more than 60 workers (8 per cent).

Table 18
Classification of Units on the Basis of Number of Skilled Workers

No. of workers	*No. of units*	*Percentage to total*
Up to 5	28	67
5-10	4	9
10 and above	10	24
Total	42	100

Out of 42 sample units about 28 units employed skilled workers up to5, 4units employed skilled workers more than 5 but less than 10 (9 per cent).

And 10 units employed 10 and more skilled workers (24per cent of the total units). It was observed that all the skilled workers employed in the sample units were male members only, no women workers employed as skilled workers.

Table 19
Main Means of Skill Acquisition

Means of skill acquisition	*Percentage to total*
Apprentice ship	45
Technical education	30
Earlier job	10
Family occupation	15
Total	100

Source: Field survey.

Among the sample units 45 per cent of total skilled workers were gone for apprentice ship. Technical education acquired 30 per cent, earlier job training 10 per cent. Those skilled workers who acquired their skill through tradition or family occupation were 15 per cent. Formal qualification s was not necessary for entry into apprentice ship. The majority of workers were formerly un-skilled at the time of appointment and they further improved their skill by working in the modern rice mills.

Out of the 42 units surveyed no unit have direct influence on the basis relationship. Majority of units i.e. 24 units (67 per cent) select skilled workers on the basis of past experience, 8 units (19 per cent) select skilled labors on the basis of their technical qualification. Only 4 units (10 per cent) gave importance to the locality-Kalady and surrounding places. They prefer to select labours on the basis proximity to the units. Only 2units selected on the basis of direct request from labourers, 4 units give importance to the quality of work.

Table 20
Distribution of Modern Rice Mill Skilled Workers on the Basis of Factors Influencing Selection

Factors influencing selection	*No. of units*	*Percentage to total*
Relationship	–	–
Past experience	24	67
Technical qualification	8	19
Proximity	4	10
Direct request by workers	2	4
Quality of work	4	10
Total	42	100

Source: Field survey

Table 21
Locality Classification of Skilled Workers

Location of skilled workers	*Percentage to total*
Local area	50
Inside the district	19
Inside the state	10
Out side the state	21
Total	100

Majority of skilled workers were selected from local area (50 per cent), 19 per cent of skilled labours were selected from inside the district of Ernakulam and10 per cent of the total skilled workers selected from inside the state of Kerala, and 21 per cent of skilled labours were selected from outside the state.

Table 22
Gender Classificaiton of Skilled Workers

Gender Classification	*Per cent*
Male Workers	100
Female Workers	–
Total	100

Table 22 shows the gender classification of skilled workers. All the skilled workers were male member. There was not a single female worker in this skilled sector of the Modern Rice Mills in and around Kalady.

Table 23
Locality Wise Classification of Unskilled labours

Location of unskilled labours	*Percentage of total*
Local area and inside the district	35
Out side the district and inside the state	10
Out side the state	55
Total	100

Source: Field survey.

Majority of the unskilled workers were from outside the state 55 per cent of the total, 35 per cent of the unskilled workers were from the local area and inside the district, where as only 10 per cent of the workers were from inside the state but out side the district. Majority of workers were from Tamilnadu, West Bengal and Orissa states.

Table 24
Classification of Modern Rice Mills on the Basis of Number of Un skilled Workers

No. of un skilled workers	*No. of units*	*Percentage to total*
Up to 10	5	12
10-20	19	45
20-30	15	36
30-40	2	4
40-50	1	3
Total	42	100

Source: Field Survey.

Classification of modern rice mills on the basis of the number of unskilled workers (loading and unloading) revealed that 5 units employed up to 10 workers, 19 units employed in between 10-20, (45 per cent), 15 units employed in between 20-30, (36 per cent), 2 units employed unskilled workers above 30 and below 40, only 1 unit employed workers in-between 40-50 category.

Table 25
Gender Classificaiton of Unskilled Workers

Gender Classification	*Per cent*
Male Workers	100
Female Workers	-
Total	100

All the workers belonged to the male category. There was not a single worker in the female catagory. This may be due to the nature of work done by the unskilled workers.

Table 26
Locality Classification of Administrative Staff of Modern Rice Mills

Locality classification of administrative staff	*Percentage*
Local area	88
Outside the local area but inside the district	8
Outside the district but inside the state	2
Out side the state	2
Total	100

Source: Field survey.

Locality classification of the administrative staff revealed that majority of the staff belonged to the local area (88 per cent of the total). Only 8 per cent of the staff belonged to the same district other than the local area. Only 2 per cent were employed from outside the district but with in the state. Only 2 per cent of the total staff were employed from outside the state.

Table 27
Factors Influencing Selection of Administrative Staff

Factors influencing selection	*Percentage*
Relation ship	23
Past experience	25
Qualification	20
Proximity	12
Direct request	20
Quality of work	-
Total	100

Source: Field Survey.

Of the 42 units surveyed, 23 per cent of the administrative staff were appointed on the basis of relationship. 25 per cent of the administrative staff were appointed on the basis of past experience. Only 20 per cent of the staff were selected purely on this basis of qualification. 12 per cent of the employees were appointed on the basis of proximity to the units. Another 20 per cent of the employees were selected on the basis of direct request.

Table 28
Educational Qualification of the Admininitrsative Staff

Educational qualification	*Percentage*
Illiterate	—
Primary education	2
Secondary education	8
Graduation	68
Post-graduation	22
Total	100

Source: Field survey.

Out of 42 units surveyed regarding the educational qualification of the administrative staff, majority of the employees were graduated, (68 per cent of the total...22 per cent of the total) staff were post- graduated, only 2 per cent of the staff have educational qualification of primary level and 8 per cent of the total staff got secondary education.

Table 29
Number of Adminstrativestaff Employed in Modern Rice Mills in and Around Kalady

Number of administrative staff	*No.of units*	*Percentage to total*
Up to 5	33	79
Between 5-10	6	14
10 and above	3	7
Total	42	100

Source: Field survey.

Out of 42 units surveyed 33 units (79 per cent) of the modern rice mills employed administrative staff up to 5 and 6 units (14 per cent) employed administrative in between 5-10. Only 3 units (7 per cent) employed 10 and above staff.

Table 30
Gender Classificaiotn of Administrative Staff

Gender Classification	*Per cent*
Male Workers	72
Female Workers	28
Total	100

Table 30 shows the Gender classification of Administrative Staff of the modern rice mills in and around Kalady. 72 per cent of the total staff belong to the male category and 28 per cent belong to the female category.

INPUT MOBILISATION PRACTICES

The development of a cluster is primarily depending up on the availability of rawmaterials for its production functior.. The main output (product) of Kalady cluster of modern rice mill is rice and allied products derived from the raw material -paddy. Paddy is the raw material of the modern rice mills in and around Kalady. This section deals with the purchase, procurement, processing etc. of paddy.

Table 31
Preference of Purchasing Paddy (Variety)

Variety of paddy	*No. of units*	*Percentage to total*
Those units which prefer 'matta' variety of paddy	42	100
Those units which do not prefer 'matta' variety of paddy	–	–
Total	42	100

Source: Field survey.

All the units reported that they have the preference for matta variety of paddy and they usually prefer " JYOTHI" variety of paddy for processing, as the kernel have little breakage and less moisture content and it has high demand from the customers. Naturally the rice mills in and around kalady have the first preference for the 'jyothi variety' of paddy.

Table 32
System of Grading

Variety of paddy	*No. of units*	*Percentage to total*
Those units have the system of grading at the time of purchasing	42	`100
Those units which do not have the system of grading at the time of purchase of paddy	–	–
Total	42	100

Source: Field survey.

All the 42 units reported that they have already the system of grading paddy (raw material) at the time of purchase. The paddy purchased by the units were usually graded as ' first quality' 'second quality' 'third quality' etc by the owners of the rice mills on the basis of moisture content of the paddy, maturity, the chaffy grains contained in the lot .

Table 33
Purchasing of Paddy on the Basis of Time at Which Samples were Shown

Process of purchasing paddy	*No. of units*	*Percentage to total*
Samples shown earlier	8	19
Samples shown at the time purchase	32	76
Both methods	2	5
Total	42	100

Source: Field survey.

Major share of rice mills (32 units) surveyed reported that they make their purchases on the basis of samples shown at the time of purchase(76 per cent).0nly 8 units (19 per cent) make their purchases on the basis samples shown earlier. Only 2 units (5per cent) makes their purchases on both the methods i.e. sample shown earlier as well as at the time of purchase.

Majority of the units under study reported that they prefer to purchase samples verified by themselves (52 per cent). 9 units prefer to purchase paddy, on the basis samples verified by representatives of the rice mill owners (21 per cent). Only 2 units (5 per cent of the total) reported that they prefer to purchase paddy on the basis samples verified by the agents of paddy vendors. 4units prefer to purchase paddy on the basis of samples verified by paddy brokers and agents of rice mill owners. Another 4units (10 per cent) reported that they used to purchase paddy on the basis of samples verified by agents of rice mill owners.

Table 34
Process of Verification of the Samples of Paddy

Verification done by	*No. of units*	*Percentage to total*
Rice mill owners	22	52
Paddy brokers	1	2
Sub brokers	–	–
Agents of paddy vendors	2	5
Representatives of rice mill owners	9	21
Paddy brokers and Agents of rice mill owners	4	10
Agent of rice mill owners	4	10
Total	42	100

Source: Field survey.

Table 35
Frequency of Purchase of Material

Frequency of purchase of paddy	*No.of units*	*Percentage to total*
Daily purchase	33	79
Alternative days	6	14
Weekly	–	–
Others (based on the requirements)	3	7
Total	42	100

Source: Field survey.

Seventy nine per cent of the units reported that they purchase the raw material (paddy) on daily basis. Only 14 per cent of the units reported that they purchase paddy on alternative days. Only 7 per cent of the units reported that they make the purchase as and when they need raw material.

Table 36
Locational Classification of Storing Raw Material

Location	*No .f units*	*Percentage to total*
Within the locality	39	93
Outside the locality	–	–
Both (within the locality as well as outside)	3	7
Total	42	100

Source: Field survey.

Ninety three per cent of the units reported (39 units) that they have their own storage facilitites with in the locality for keeping raw material. Only 3 units reported that they have storage facilities inside the locality as well out side the locality. Majority of the units keep their raw material near to their production centre.

Table 37
Sources of Procurement of Paddy by Modern Rice Mills

Sources of procurement of paddy	*No. of units*	*Percentage to total*
With in the district only	1	2
Outside the district but with in the state	4	10
With in and out side the district	6	14
Out side the state only	3	7
Out side the district but with in the state and outside the state	12	29
With in and outside the district and outside the state	7	17
Outside the district but with in the state with in and outside the district	2	5
With in the district, outside the district but within in the state and outside the state	3	6
With in the district and outside state	4	10
Total	42	100

Source: Field survey.

Twenty nine per cent of the units reported that they were purchasing the paddy from outside the district but with in the state and outside the state, 17 per cent of the mills procure paddy from with in and out side the district and outside the state. 14 per cent of the units procure paddy from with in and outside the district . 10 per cent of the units purchases paddy from outside the district .10 per cent of the units purchases paddy from outside the district but with in the state. Another 10 per cent procure paddy within the district and outside the state. 7 per cent of the units procure paddy from outside the state alone. 5 per cent of the units procure paddy outside the district but with in thee state, with in and outside the district. Majority of rice mills in and around kalady depends for paddy (raw material) from outside the state. This is evident from the Table 4 (33) that the modern rice mills inand around Kalady is not getting enough paddy for processing with in the state of Kerala, because t of the sharp decline trend in paddy cultivation.

Table 38
Factors Affecting Price Determination of Paddy

Factors affecting price determination	*No. of units*	*Percentage to total*
Quality of paddy	28	67
Place of origin	–	–
Period of credit	3	7
Quality and period of credit	5	12
Quality demand and period of credit	6	14
Other factors		

Sources: Field survey.

Majority of rice mills (67 per cent) purchases paddy from cultivators on the basis of the quality of the paddy . No unit gives importance to the place of origin of the paddy. 3 units (7 per cent) revealed that they gives importance to the period of credit allowed. Only 12 per cent of the units gives importance to the quality and period of credit taken together. only 6 units (14 per cent) gives importance to the quality, demand and credit factors.

Table 39
Ranking of Main Suppliers of Paddy (state wise)

Name of state	*Rank*
Tamil nadu	I
Karnataka	II
Maharastra	III
Uttar pradesh	IV
Madhya pradesh	V
Kerala	VI
Punjab	VII
Andhrapradesh	VIII

Source: Field survey.

The 42 units reported that for rawmaterial, they depend on neighbouring states like Tamilnadu,Karnataka, Maharastra, UP, MP, and even for Punjab and Andhra Pradesh, even though

Andhra Pradesh is producing too much paddy, they are not supplying paddy, but they are supplying processed rice to the state of Kerala. In Kerala the production of paddy is very low as it is sufficient for less than 11 per cent of the total requirement. The reasons for law productivity are being analysed in detail in chapter 5.

Table 40
Availability of Storage Facility for Procuring Paddy by the Modern Rice Mills

Storage facility	*No of units*	*Percentage to total*
Those rice mills which have the storage facility	42	100
Those rice mills which do not have the storage facility	–	–
Total	42	100

Source: Field survey.

All the 42 units surveyed have the storage facility.

Table 41
Storage Capacity of Modern Rice Mills

Storage capacity	*No. of units*	*Percentage to total*
Less than 50 tonne	2	5
50-100 Tonne	8	19
101-250 Tonne	9	21
251-500 Tonne	6	14
500-1000 Tonne	12	29
Above 1000 Tonnes	5	12
Total	42	100

Source : Field survey
* 10 tonnes =1 lorry load.

Only 2 units have (5 per cent of the total) less than 50 tonnes storage capacity, twelve units have (29 per cent) storage capacity varying from 501–1000 tonnes. 6 units have storage capacity up to 500 tonnes. 8 units have storage capacity in between 50-100 tonnes. Only 5 units have storage capacity of above 1000 tonnes.

Table 42
Price Fixers of Paddy

Price fixers of paddy	*No of units*	*Percentage to total*
Paddy brokers	6	14
Rice mill owners	25	59
Agents of rice mill owners	3	7
Paddy brokers of rice mill owners	9	20
Farmers	–	–
Others	–	–
Total	42	100

Source: Field survey.

Table 42 revealed that the price of paddy was fixed by the owners of rice mills (59 per cent). Nine units reported that the price of paddy was fixed by paddy brokers appointed by the rice mill owners. Six units reported that the price of paddy was fixed by paddy brokers alone. It is very intresting that the farmers have no role in fixing the price of paddy.

Table 43
Method of Purchasing Paddy

Method of purchasing paddy	*No. of units*	*Percentage to total*
Bulk purchase of paddy	40	95
Purchase by samples	2	5
Purchase by advertisements	–	–
Total	42	100

Source: Field survey.

Majority of rice mills in Kalady reported that they were making bulk purchase of paddy, (95 per cent). Only 2 units (5 per cent) purchased paddy by samples.

Table 44
Co-operation among Modern Rice Mills in Procuring Paddy

Co-operation among rice mills in procuring paddy	*No. of units*	*Percentage to total*
Those who co- operate with other ricee mills	22	52
Those who partially co–operate with other rice mills	10	24
Those who do not co-operate with other mills	10	24
Total	42	100

Source: Field survey

Among the 42 units reported 22 units were fully cooperating with each other in procuring paddy from the cultivators of paddy. Another 10 units reported that the were partially co-operating, and remaining 10 units reported that they did no co–operate with other units in procuring paddy from the cultivators.

Table 45
Methods for Price Determination of Paddy

Method of price determination	*No of units*	*Percentage to total*
Open bargaining between paddy vendors and rice mill owners	3	7
Secret negotiation between paddy vendors and rice mill owners	2	4
Public auction	1	2
Open / secret negotiation between paddy brokers and rice mill owners	19	45
Open /secret negotiation between paddy brokers, vendor, and rice mill owners	6	14
Through auction, open/secret negotiation with paddy broker, vendors, rice millowners	4	9
Through auction, open/ secret negotiation between paddy brokers and paddy endors	8	19
Total	42	100

Source: Field survey.

Among the 42 units, 19 units revealed that (45 per cent) they purchase paddy by open/secret negotiation between paddy broker and rice mill owners. Only 6 units (14 per cent) reported that the method of price determination by open/ secret negotiation between paddy vendor, paddy broker, and rice mill owners. Only 8 units (19 per cent) fix the price through auction, open/secret negotitation between paddy brokers and paddy vendors.

Majoiry of units 28 units (67 per cent) availed a credit period of 15 days from the suppliers of paddy. It was also revealed that credit practice was followed by all units taken as sample units. Eight units reported that (19 per cent),they

Table 46
Details Regarding the Credit Period Allowed by Suppliers of Paddy

Period of credit	*No .of units*	*Percentage*
No credit	–	–
Up to 15 days	28	67
Up to 30 days	8	19
Up to 60 days	3	7
60 days and above	3	7
Total	42	100

Source: Field survey.

availed a period of 30 days from the suppliers of paddy. Only 3units (7per cent) had the practice of credit period upto 60 days(two months) and another 3 units reported that (7 per cent) get the credit period of more than 60 days from the suppliers of paddy.

Table 47
Basis of Payment of Brokerage/Commission

Method of payment	*No of units*	*Percentage to toal*
Brokerage/commission paid as a percentage of the procurement price of paddy	4	10
Brokerage/commission per lorry load	36	85
Brokerage/commission paid on daily	2	5
Total	42	100

Source: Field survey.

Majoriry of rice mills in Kalady, ie. 36 units (85 per cent) paid brokerage/commission on the basis of the lorry load .Only 4 units (10 per cent) paid on the basis of percentage on the procurement price of the paddy. Only 2 units surveyed were reported to have observed payment of brokerage/commission to the paddy brokers for purchasing paddy.

FORWARD LIKAGES OF MODERN RICE MILLS IN AND AROUND KALADY

The forward linkage of rice and its effects to the community received much attention due to its economic and social benefits to the community. An attempt to have discussion with regard to some aspects of the forward linkages among the sample units. Information were gathered in the beginning of the businsess and in the current year (2003 -04). The main output of the modern rice mills are 'mattarice'-'rice bran' and husk are by products of the rice mill business.The rice mill industry in and around Kalady is mainly concentrated on the main product– mattarice'. At present there is one rice bran extraction unit in Kalady. The KaladyRice millers consortium (KRMC) is a cluster of 39 rice mills operating in and around Kalady. It is running a project to extract crude rice bran oil and refined oil (edible) at Kalady.

Table 48
Technique of Product Differenciation Introducers

Name of performers	*No of units*	*Percentage to total*
Owners	34	81
Owners and workers	6	14
Experts fromlocal area	–	–
Experts from out side	–	–
Experts from inside and outside	–	–
Own workers and experts from inside and outside	2	
Total	42	100

Out of 42 units surveyed 34 units revealed that (81 per cent) the technique of product differenciation was performed by owners of modern rice miils. Six units reported that this function is done by owners and workers together. Only 2 units seek the help of own workers, and experts from inside and out side the locality.

Table 49
Introducers of Product Innovation

Introducers of innovation	*No of units*	*Percentage to total*
Owners and workers	6	14
Owners alone	32	76
Experts out side the local area	–	–
Experts from inside and outside the local area	2	5
Owners, workers, and experts from local and outside the locality	2	5
Total	42	100

Source: Field survey.

It was proved from the Table 49 that majority of product innovation of modern rice mills in and around kalady were observed to be done by the owners (76 per cent) . Only 6 units (14 per cent) revealed that innovation techniques were applied by rice millowners and workers together. Only 2 units exercised the practice with the help of experts from inside the locality and outside the area. Another 2 units (5 per cent) expressed that the work was done by owners, experts from with in the locality and outside the locality.

Table 50
Decision Takers in the Price of the Product

Persons fix the price of the product	*No of units*	*Percentage to total units*
Experts in this field	–	–
Experts in side the locality and outside	–	–
Own workers and experts in the local area	–	–
Own workers and experts out side the local area	–	–
Owners of rice mills	–	–
Own workers, experts inside and ouside the locality	42	100
Total	42	100

Source: Field survey.

The surveyed units reported that the determination of the price of the product was determined by the owners of rice mills in kalady, consideringvarious market factors.

Table 51
Persons Responsible for Market Strategies

Persons responsible for market strategies	*No .of units*	*Percentage to total*
Own workers	19	2
Experts in the local area	12	45
Experts out side the local area	6	14
Own workers, experts in the local area	–	–
Experts in the ocal area and outside the local area	–	–
Owners of rice mills and own workers	5	12
Total	42	100

Source: Field survey.

Market strategies, were designed by experts from the local area in the 45 per cent of the units. Only 19 per cent of market strategies designed by workers of rice mills. These work were done by experts in the local area, 14 per cent of the total units surveyed reported that these works were done by experts out side the locality. Another 12 per cent of the units reported that, market strategies, advertisements etc. were done jointly by the owners of rice mills and their own workers.

Table 52

Details of Market Arrangements of Modern Rice Mills in Kalady

(in percentage)

Details	*Direct to customer*	*Retailers*	*Whole salers*	*Sales executives*	*Outlets*	*Total (Percentnge)*
Sales in the beginning	12	48	38	2	–	100
Sales in the current year	7	57	29	5	2	100

Source: Field survey.

Table 52 gives the details of marketing arrangements of modernrice mills in and around Kalady. Marketing through retailers was a dominant form of market strategy, 48 per cent of sales in the beginning period and 57 per cent in the current year sales were made through retailers. Another important form of market strategy was whole salers. In the begining it was 38 per cent of total sales and 29 per cent in the current year. It was also an encouraging factor that sales through their own outlets shows an increasing trend.

Table 53

Details Regarding Area of Sales by Reporting Units

Details of area	*Percentage of sales*
Local area	6
With inErnakulamdistrict other than local area	10
Rest of the state of Kerala	65
Outside the state of Kerala	11
Outside the country	8
Total	100

Source: Field survey.

Table 53 shows that 6 per cent of the sales were made in the local area, and another 10 per cent sales were made in the home district. Major share of sales, 65 per cent were made in the rest of Kerala. Eleven per cent sales were made in other parts of the country, predomninantly used by 'malayalees'. It was also reported that therewas an export potential of 8 per cent of total sales, this also used by Malayalees.

Table 54
Marketing Intensity of Various Categories of Rice Available in different Packets

Different packets	*Percentage*	*Rank*
10 kg packets	40	I[st]
75 kg packets	28	IInd
25 kg packets	23	IIIrd
50 kg packets	6.5	IVth
100 kg packets	2.5	V[th]
Total	100	

Source: Field survey.

Major share of sales of the reporting units were 10 kg packets which was 40 per cent of the total sales matta rice in Kerala. Another category of 75 kg packets constitute 28 per cent of sales. Twenty five kg bags were shown 23 percentage on total sales, where as 50 kg bags showed only a sale 6.5 per cent. 100 kg bags showed a sale of 2.5 per cent of total sales which ranks last.

Table 55
Intensity of Demand of Variety of Matta Rice

Variety of rice	*Fast moving*	*Slowmoving*	*Deadly slow moving*	*Total No.*
Matta (Bold) rice[1]	33(79)	9(21)	–	42 (100)
Matta(Vadi) rice[2]	37 (88)	5(12)	–	42 (100)
Other Varieties of rice	3 (7)	26 (62)	13 (31)	42 (100)

Source: Field survey

(Figures in the paranthesis represent percentage)

1 Bold rice-round shaped brownish coloured variey of rice

2 Vadi rice-long and brownish coloured variety of rice

Table 55 shows that on the basis of different variey of rice, the 'Bold rice' was the fast moving item of 33 units (79 per cents of the sales), where as in 9 units it was a slow moving item (21 per cent). In the case of 'Vadi rice' in 37 units (88 per cent) it is fast moving item where as in 5 units reported it was a slow moving item . In other varieties of rice 3 units reported that it was fast moving item and 26 units a slow moving item and 13 units it is deadly slow moving item.

Table 56
Details of Credit Period Allowed to Customers of Modern Rice Mills

	No of units	*Percentage to total units*
No credit	2	5
Up to 15 days	31	74
Up to 30 days	9	21
Up to 60 days	—	—
60 days and above	—	—
Total	42	100

Source: field survey.

Majority of units 31 (74 per cent) reported that they were providing 15 days credit. Only 9 units (21per cent) reported that they were providing one month credit period. All the units were allowing credit to the customers except 2 units (5per cent). No unit reported credit period upto 60 days or above 60 days. 2 units reported that they were entertaining only cash transactions.

Table 57
Classification of Modern Rice Mills on the Basis of Mode of Advertisement

Method of advertisement	*No of units*	*Percentage to toal*
News paper and periodicals	5	12
Radio	3	7
Cable net work TV s	5	12
Slides in the cinema theatre	6	14
Hoardings	4	10
Wall advertisements	-	-
Flux board advertisements	8	19
Calendar and other printed materials	3	7
Other means of advertisements	5	12
Other means of advertisements	3	7
Total	42	100

Source: Field survey.

Nineteen per cent of the reported units depends mainly on wall advertisements, 14per cent depends on cable net work TVs as the main media of advertisement, 10 per cent of the units depends on sides in the cinema theatres, 12 per cent depends on calendar and other print ed materials.

COMPETION AMONG MODERN RICE MILL IN AND AROUND KALADY

Cluster of rice mills in and around Kalady realized the need for collaboration among one another and equally important is the need to compete one another. Inerviews with the owners of sample units revealed that there exist cut-throat competition between the units in terms of product design, and process innovation, marketing the product etc. A few units follwed un ethical practices against helthy competition among the sample units.

Table 58
Competitive Strategy of Modern Rice Mills in and Around Kalady

Strategies resorted to by units	*No. of units*	*Percentage to total*
Imitation of products design		–
Advertisements		13
Imitating trade marks		4
Marketing methods		52
Recruiting labours from better placed units		16
Other un ethical practices		15
Total		100

Table 59
Details of Joint–business Activities of the Modern Rice Mills in and Around Kalady

Joint –business activity	*No. of units*	*Percentage to total*
Those who fully involved in joint business activities	32	76
Those who are partially involved in joint business activities	4	10
Those who are not interested in joint business activities	3	7
Those who are interested in joint business activities	3	7
Total	42	100

Source: Field survey

On the basis of Table 59 the surveyed units reported that 32 units were (76 per cent) already involved in joint- business activities. Another 4 units (10 per cent) reported that they were partially involved in joint- business activities . only 3 units reported that they were not interested in joint business activities. Another 3 units (7 per cent) reported that they were interested in joint–business activities.

Table 60
Details of Business Relations with in the Cluster of Modern Rice Mills in Kalady

Details of relation ship	*No of units*	*Percentage to total*
Those who have good business relation with other units	32	76
Thoe who have partial relations with other units	6	14
Those who donot have any business relation with other units	4	10
Total	42	100

Source: Field survey.

Majority of the units (32)reported that they have strong relations with other units in the cluster (76 per cent of the units). But 4 units repotrted that they have no relation with other units. 6 units reported that they have prtial relations with other units (14 per cent).

Table 61
Details of Membership of Associations

Name of association	*No. of units*	*Percentage to total*
Kerala Rice Mill Owners association	42	100
Total	42	100

Source: Field survey.

All the units reported that they were maintaining membership in the sole association ie. Kerala rice mill owners association, which is functioning state level as wellas district basis.

It was revealed by the units that majority of them (52 per cent of the units) have co-operation in purchasing raw material(paddy) for this purpose, they have organized a paddy open market yard at Mattoor, Kalady. Another 10 units (24

Table 62
Details of Inter- firm Linkages With in the Cluster of Modern Rice Mills in and Around Kalady

Details of activities of linkage	*No of units*	*Percentage to total*
Joint-recruitment/selection of new workers	–	–
Joint- search for new markets	2	5
Sharing of spare capacity, storage facilities, technicians, experts etc.	2	5
Exchange of technology, ideas of management etc.	3	7
Joint- purchasing of raw materials (paddy)	22	52
Sharing of transport facilities	–	–
Details of activities of linkage	*No of units*	*Percentage to total*
Joint- marketing of products	–	–
Joint-venture of by products marketing	10	24
Joint efforts of Research and Development(R&D)	–	–
Joint–purchasing of plant & machineries, and equipments	3	7
Total	42	100

Source: Field survey.

per cent) have formed a syndicate to market thire by products mainly rice bran . Two units have efforts towards joint search for raw material. 3 units have co-operated in purchasing machineries and equipments. The paddy pen market yard is operated and controlled by Rice Mill Owners Association and Kalady Rice Millers Consortium jointly. More than 120 lorry loads paddy come in to the market every day. The total transactions amounting to Rs. 2.5 crores on an average per day. This is one of the biggest paddy market in Kerala. The benefits of clustering are being enjoyed by almost all surveyed units in terms of purchase, production and marketing of rice which again acts as a boost to cluster rice mills in Kalady.

Table 63 revealed that majority of modern rice mills in and around Kalady is getting services from the rice mill owners association in raw material procurement, efforts for improving infrastructural facilities utilization of by product by forming a consortium of ricemills called Kalady Rice Millers Consortium– mainly concenterated in utilizing by products such as rice bran, paddy husk . Theyare also rendering services such as lobbying with the government of Kerala and central government in matters related to tax issues and general issues.They are also taking the main role in solving trade related issues such as labour problem material shortage etc.

Table 63
Responses of Modern Rice Mills in Kalady According to Services Received from Kerala Rice Mill Owners Association

Name of service	*Permanent*	*Temprory*	*Never*	*Total units*
Solutions to labour problems	22	13	7	42
Raw material management	32	8	2	42
Advice on legal matters	10	20	12	42
Lobbying with the government	30	8	4	42
Discouraging un ethical practice	-	-	-	42
Conducting seminars, workshops for tax related issues	20	21	1	1
Formation of price policies, market strategy etc.	23	9	10	42
Efforts for improving infra-structural facilities	29	9	4	42
Utilisation of by products	32	9	1	42
Product innovations	—	8	34	42

Source: Field survey.

Table 64
Responses of the Modern rice Mills in Kalady about the Advantages of Clustering of Rice Mill Units in and Around Kalady

Advantages	*No . of units*	*Percentage to total units*
Availability of raw material	32	76
Availability of cheap labour	5	12
Availability of transport and communication facilities	9	21
Availability of technical know how	8	19
Conducting courses and seminars	33	79
Training programmes for quqlity improvement	8	19
Jont- arbitration in disputes	12	29
Developing common facility centre	9	21
Native place advantage	32	76
Proximity to problem solving instituitions	23	55
Lobbying with the government agencies	29	69

Source: Field survey.

All the units surveyed expressed their satisfaction in developing a cluster of modern rice in and around Kalady.

Table 65
Distribution of Units According to their Views to Improve the Performance of the Cluster of Modern Rice Mill Units in and Around Kalady

Suggestions	*No. of units*	*Percentage to total units*
Assuring supply of rawmaterial (paddy)	42	100
Assuring better infrastructural facilities	42	100
More technology centres	13	31
Availability of cheap labour	28	67
More tax incentives	42	100
Better credit facilities at cheaper rate of interest	42	100
Support of governments	42	100

Source: Field survey.

New inititatives suggested by the modern rice mills in and around Kalady as the steps necessary for improving the performance of cluster were listed in Table 65. All the units suggested the smooth supply of raw material (paddy) through out the year. Better infrastructural facilities such as supply of electricity, transport facilities etc. also to be improved. More tax incentives and support from government agencies are also necessary for cluster development . There is also the need for better and cheap credit facilities for staring new units in this locality.

Table 66
Responses of Units According to Their Perception on the Future of the Cluster

Future trends	*No of units*	*Percentage total*
Modern rice mill units will grow	29	69
Units will remain unchanged	11	26
Units will decline	2	5
Total	42	100

Source: Field survey.

Of the 42 units surveyed, 29 units (69 per cent) have the opinion of bright future of modern rice mills in and around Kalady and they expressed the hope that the rice mill business and its cluster will have bright future. Only 11 units have the opinion that they will remain unchanged for the years to come (26 per cent). Two units expressed their dismay regarding the rice processing industry in Kalady.

KERALA MODEL OF CLUSTERING

Kalady Rice Millers Consortium is formed as a private limited company, consisting 39 rice mill owners in and around Kalady as its members. Its authorised and paid up capital is RS. 2 crores and Rs 30 lakh as margin money loan (MML) from the Government of Kerala through Development Commissioner Small Scale Industries (DCSSI). The administration of the consortium is vested with the Board of Directors elected From the rice mill owners (share holders), They together elect a Managing Director, to look after the day to day affairs of the consortium.

The rice mill cluster in and around Kalady has a total production capacity of (2005) of about 2000 metric tonnes of par boiled rice per day .The annual capacity is more than 600,000 metric tonnes of par boiled rice . In addition to this the rice mills produce 300 metric tonnes of rice bran per day-annual production of about 90,000metric tonnes. Rice bran can use to extract rice bran oil, which is called "the heart oil or healthy oil". This is a very good cooking medium. It contains useful functional food un saturated fatty acid. It also contains high vitamin E it improves the blood circulation. Even though the commercial value of rice bran is very high, the rice mill units did not get adequate price for their by products. Rice bran is a highly sensitive product s and its quality deteriorate while storing . High quality oil is extracted only from fresh bran. Oils in bran contain some free fatty acids. The enzymatic hydrolysis goes on storing them and leads to rancidity. To avoid this bran is made to process with in 2 or 3 days from their production.

COMMON FACILITY CENTRE EXPELLER

Earlier the rice mills in Kalady (cluster) were only involved in operations related to de husking of paddy and polishing rice.

There was not a single unit in Kerala to extract rice bran oil, there fore rice bran was neither polished neither by cluster members nor by enterprises in the state of Kerala. It was sold to middle men for processing in the adjoining states like Karnataka, Tamilnadu etc. In order to utilise the rice bran, KRMC (Kalady rice millers consortium) established a major plant at Kalady to tap the un- utilised rice bran so that they will get maximum price for their by products. Product and market development initiative have included establishment of a common brand for a quota of out put of consortium members. "Leads" is the common brand promoted by the consortium members. The CFC expeller at its full capacity will earn Rs. 2000 per member units per day, and the project will yield a benefit of Rs.6lakh per member units .Thirty nine member units can earn about Rs 2.34 crores per annum. The pay back period of the CFCexpeller unit is estimated at one and a half year. The consortium is exploring new market channels in addition to the existing channels; they plan to sell through the 'kudumbasree units'. The women members in these units can operate with in small territories around their place of domicile and pursue door to door marketing of cluster products. Further they plans to establish a refinery unit whch will help to increase realisation of more value added product from the expelling plant is expected.

Learning important lessons from the successful experience of the Rubber Footwear Industry at Kottayam and securing support from the Development Commissioner Of Small Scale Industries (DCSSI) . The establishment of Rice Bran Oil extraction Unit serves as an illustration on crystalisation of joint- business activities of rice mill cluster in Kalady.The KRMC is a member of the 'All India Solvent Extractors Association (S.E.A). A common packaging facility has also been established. This will also facilitate production of appropriate material for packing rice bran oil.

COMMON TESTING LABORATORY

A laboratory for testing rice bran oil, rice, rice bran and other products of the member units is established at Kalady .This laboratory offers all the facilities offered by other similar laboratories in this field. This is a good step towards product innovation and designing. The rice mills in Kalady were depending up on private owned laboratories mainly located at Kochi about—kilometers away from Kalady.The charges of common testing laboratory is very cheap when compared to private laboratories, so that each member can save Rs 50,000 per year. The effective pay back period of this project is less than one year.

COMMON CONSUMABLE STORE

The Consortium has established a common storage facility with administration office facilities for purchase of 'mill stores' (viz. gears, shafts, and belt drives) and rubber tyres for trucks and Light Commercial Vehicles (LCV's) are directly purchased from manufacturers. Consumables are purchased from manufacturers /fabricators and importers (bearings from China). This facility is directly managed by specially trained staff. Other 'mill stores' items include pulley, and rubber and nylon conveyer belts etc. are purchased from Coimbatore. A revolving fund of Rs .5 lakh is used as working capital exclusively for this purpose. The activity of common purchase facility helps rice mills to secure discounts varying from 8-30% for different products. The KRMC operates on gross profit margin of 2%. Net margins after salaries and expenses are 0.5%.Net profits are retained in the consortium. By operating this facility member unit in the cluster saves an average about 15% on the cost of various consumables. In addition a sum of Rs.2.5 lakh is used for procuring tyres (in pooled quantities) directly from manufacturers.

PADDY OPEN MARKET YARD

In 2004, the consortium established a well developed common market yard at Kalady. About 120 lorry loads of paddy from different parts of the country on an average come in the open market yard everyday. Trade is estimated Rs 2.5 crores per day. Different cropping patterns and seasonality even with in Kerala ensures that this facility is operational round the year.

The Paddy Open Market facilitates procurement and storage of paddy, in order to avoid the shut down of rice mills for want of paddy (raw-material). Moreover the farmers can very wellavoidmiddlemen and to get fair prices for their product. This paddy open market is very first of its kind in paddy-rice system in India.

TRAINING PROGRAMMES

Various training programmes including a 3 month duration is conducted for the skilled as wellas semi-skilled employees of the member units. These training programmes are co-sponsored by Rice Mill Owners Association, SIDBI, etc.

ENCOURAGE THE FARMERS FOR APPROPRIATE CROPPING PATTERN

The Consortium with the collaborations of the Pattambi Rice Research Station (RRS), launch a Programme to encourage farmers to shift to High Yielding Rice Varieties. The support and help from Kerala Agricultural University is also solicited to help farmers .The rice mill units in Kalady realised the need for the survival of paddy cultivation in Kerala,which is declining year by year. They are also felt the need for registration under the Geographical Indications Act for specific rice varieties. The rice miller's consortium is planning to take paddy fields for 'cluster farming'.

BIO-FUEL PLANT IN PROGRESS

Establishment of captive power plants independent Bio-Gas operated generator sets are being explored as to reduce cost of power. Consortium members are exploring options progressively move in to adding value to the products. Edible oil as wellas by products may be processed in to several products. Each individual unit on an average incurs an expenditure Rs. 2.5 lakh per annum as electric city related expenses. Installation of bio-gasfiers are in progress in the Kalady cluster of rice mills.

SUPPORING INDUSTRIES OF RICE MILL CLUSTER IN KALADY-FORWARD LINKAGE

Jute Bag Manufacturing Industry

The rice mill cluster in Kalady depends very much on jute bag manufacturing for supplying packing materials. The rice mills in and around Kalady supplies matta rice in different packets of 10Kg, 25Kg, 50Kg, 75Kg, and 100Kg . All these packets used either plastic or jute bag. For environmental reasons jute bags are used by majority rice mill units in and around Kalady. Majority of rice mills in Kalady depend jute bags as packing material, which is 'ecofriendly'. The jute bag industry has units in Kalady, Okkal, Malayatoor Neeleswaram, Koovappady, Rayamngalam, Grama panchayths and Perumbavoor municipality. Majority of the jute bag industries are registerd under small scale industrial units (SSI units). Majority of the jute bag industrial units are formed as partnership and proprietary ship. There is not a single unit owned and operated either by co-operative sector or government sector. Majority of the jute bag manufacturing units in and around Kalady is working about 75 per cent of the capacity utilisation. In jute bag industrial units male as well as female labourers are working. This in turn gives employment oppertunity to large number of people.

An average investment of Rs.10 lakh is required for staring a jute bag manufacturing unit. The raw material for this industry is obtained from West Bengal. Raw material shortage, lack of skilled workers, unhealthy competition, unstable prices, of raw materials etc. are the main problems faced by these industry.

Weigh Bridge Operating Business

In Kalady and surrounding places there is concentration of weigh bridges. More than 30 weighbridges are operating in this area. Their main business is weighing paddy (raw material) for the rice mill units in and around Kalady.The average investment per Weigh Bridge is more than 6 to 8 lakhs.Their business is mainly seasonal in nature. Some of the weigh bridge centers are offering rice packets of different mills on the road side. By selling rice and rice products the weigh bridge owners are also getting additional benefits.

Kerala State Electricity Board (KSEB)

The total power requirement of each unit is approximately 160HP and thereby LT electricity connection is necessary for each unit. Since all the units are working as SSI unit so the KSEB is supplying electricity in minimum guaranteed scheme. Each unit is incurring on an average Rs. 5lakh as electricity charges. For drying the par boiled rice in drier an uninterrupted power supply is necessary.

Fuel Suppliers

Since all the units require uninterrupted power supply for all the process. But naturally there may be interruption due to various reasons. In order to avoid shut down of production process. All the units in the cluster area in stalled their own parallel power generating system operated by the use of diesel as fuel. Each unit on an average spends Rs.50000 for fuel charges (diesel charges). The diesel pumps in and around Kalady is no doubt a supporting industry to the modern rice mill cluster.

Man Power Supply

At present the rice mill cluster in and around gives employment to above 4000 persons directly and 2000 persons indirectly. There are manpower suppliers in this sector. There is shortage of skilled workers. In order to overcome this problem the rice miller's consortium is conducting training programmes to the workers.

Financial Institutions

The entire units in the Kalady rice mill cluster are depend up on the commercial banks and other financial institutions like KFC, KSIDC, SIDBI, NSIC etc. The commercial banks and financial institutions are also prospering as the modern rice mills in and around Kalady are performing well and thereby, these institutions are ready to finance the proposed expansion projects of the modern rice mill cluster.

Transport Contractors and Vehicle Dealers

The rice mill owners association and Kalady rice miller's consortium jointly operating a paddy open market at Kalady. Nowa day's paddy cultivators from different parts of the country come to the open market yard for selling paddy at reasonable prices. About 120 lorry loads come in to the yard every day. More than 150 vehicles on an average ply in between Kalady and other distant places for supplying rice and rice products though out the state and outside the state. The prosperity of rice mill cluster also help the vehicle dealers and transport contractors to a large extend.

Cattle Feed Industries

The main by product of rice mill cluster is the rice bran. The rice bran after extracting crude rice bran oil is used as cattle feed. The supply of rice bran is very much depend on the existence of cattle feed factories operating near to Kalady. The Kerala Feeds, K.S cattle feeds, MILMA etc. depend to a large extend to the rice mill cluster for their rice bran requirement, which is their raw material.

According to Porter a cluster is a group of firms engaged in particular product market in a particular location. The competitive environment for small scale agri- food business in developing countries like India is dramatically altered in recent years. The new environment characterised by globalisation, liberalisation and intensive organisational, institutional and technological change. This is cent per cent proved in the case of modern rice mill cluster in and around Kalady. By going through various phases of the development of this cluster. From house hold level to a complete modernisation and mechanisation level led to an industrial level of production and also the application of modern management and marketing technology etc.

Porter's Diamond theory of cluster proposes for inter-related facts, each of which representing a determinant of

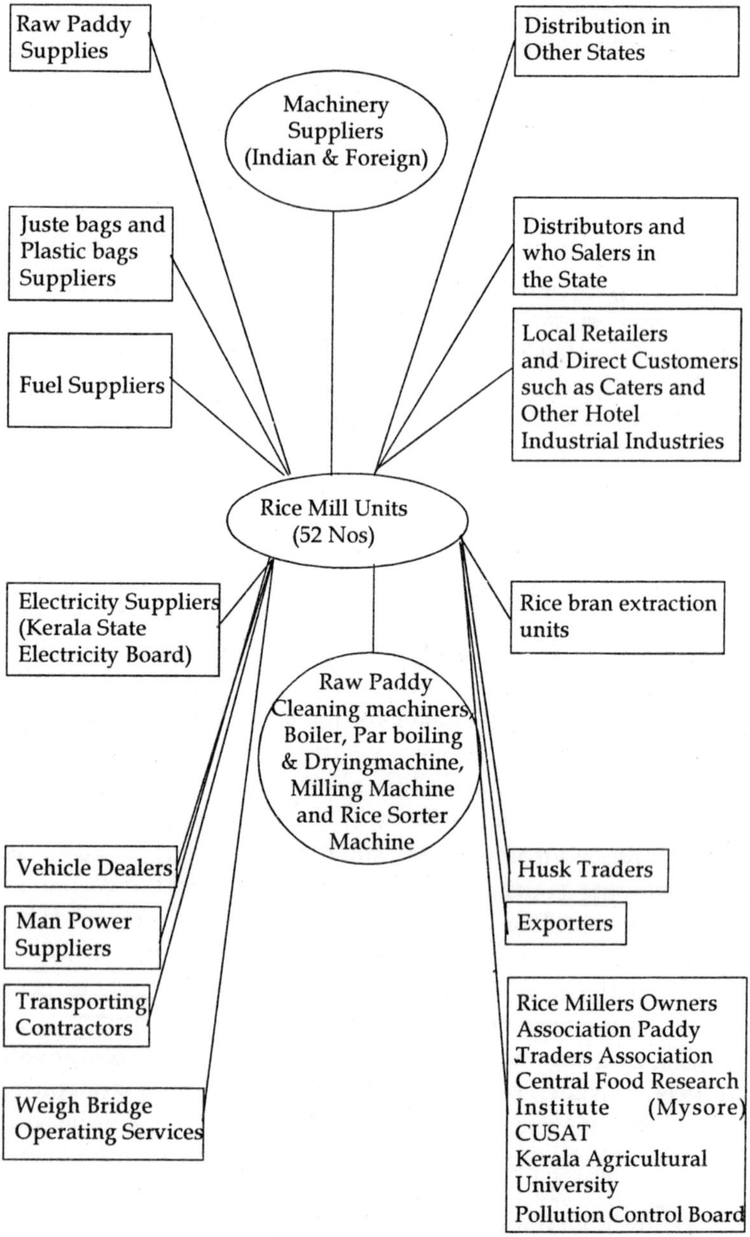

Figure 2: **Forward and Backward Linkages of Kalady Rice Mills- Cluster Map**

regional or localised advantage. The availability of pure water from the perennial water source of the river Periyar is one of the important localised factors that really influenced the clustering of modern rice mills in and around Kalady. This cluster leads to the inter related group of firms or units and institutions in a particular field of activity (rice processing) in a particular area (in and around Kalady). Porter's theory also highlight another important feature of the cluster, is value creation and value addition. This process starts from the stage of purchasing paddy for processing and after that value creation and addition of the main product (rice) as wellas by product. The stone less rice technology, sortex rice technology, extraction of rice bran oil ("Leads" Brand) through a Common Facility Centre rice bran extraction unit, a common effluent treatment plant, Fly Ash Brick factory, Bio-Fuel plant (in progress) etc.are very good examples of value creation and addition. So Malady rice millers cluster also satisfies an important feature of Porter's Diamond Theory of cluster.

Another important characteristic feature of rice miller's cluster in and around Kalady is the firm's strategies and rivalry factor conditions and demand conditions of related and supporting industries. Each modern rice mill in the cluster area plans their own market strategy of selling their main products as wellas by products. Each unit in the cluster sells their product using their own brand name and the use of individual marketing techniques.

Porter states that growth requires a dynamic co-operation to build market channels or to improve production technology. The supporting industries in this rice mill cluster of Kalady such as ;Jute bag manufacturing industry, Weigh bridge operating service, power supply unit (KSEB), man power supply agencies, financial institutions, transport contractors and vehicle dealers, cattle feed industries etc. are the main supporting and benefit deriving industries in this area. The development of those industries depends up on the improvement of rice mill cluster in and around Kalady. Porter's Diamond Theory is also applicable to these industries existence and survival.

The role of the government of Kerala and its various agencies seem to have been very significant in promoting the modern rice mill cluster in and around Kalady. Porter's Diamond Theory is fully applicable to the growth and development of modern rice mill cluster in and around Kalady.

Porter states that "clusters not only red uce transactions cost and boost efficiency but improve incentives and create collective assets in the form of information, specialised institution and reputation among others. More important clusters enable innovations and speed productivity growth".

The clustering of rice mills in and around Kalady is highly related to Entrepreneurial growth and availability of pure water (ie locational factors). To test this the hypothesis formulated is: There is positive relationship between entrepreneurial growth and availability of pure water resulting in the clustering of rice mills in and around Kalady (H1) The null hypothesis is : There is no positive relationship between entrepreneurial growth and availability pure water resulting in the cluster of rice mills in and around Kalady.

The raw material (Paddy) for this industry is mainly procured from other states. Only less than 15 per cent of total requirement of paddy is procured from Kerala. Quality of rice is decided mainly by the quality of paddy available and by the polable soft water availability for processing. Six hundred liters of waste water is generated while processing 1 metric tonne of paddy. So the availability water resources is an important factor for the installation of modern rice mills. Availability of pure water is one of the reasons for the clustering of rice mills along with entrepreneurial growth over the years. The hypothesis tested based in these variables fully confirms the relationship. Test results are given in tables 4.70 and 4.71.

The clustering of rice mills are identified on the basis of Porters Diamond Model of Clustering.

There are two locational factors that led to the concentration and conglomeration of (Clustering) of rice mills in and around Kalady. They are:

1. The entrepreneurial growth is greater in Kalady than Palakkad (all other places of concentration).

2. Availability of pure water is greater in Kalady than that of Palakkad.

Table 68
Locational Factors in Palakkad

	Enough	*Satisfactory*	*Not Satis factory*	*Total*
Entrepreneurial Growth	8	10	2	20
Availability of pure water	5	3	12	20

Sorce: Field survey.

Table 69
Locational Factors in Kalady

	Enough	*Satisfactory*	*Not Satisfactory*	*Total*
Entrepreneurial growth	32	8	2	42
Availability of pure water	42	–	–	42

Source: Field survey.

The t-value of 2.785 (for Entrepreneurial growth), and t value 4.722 (for availability of pure water) are greater than the table value and the null hypothesis is rejected. Hence the study concludes that there is a positive relationship between entrepreneurial growth and availability of pure water.

Table 70
1. Entrepreneurship is Greater in Kalady Than That of Palakkad

Test for proportion

Category	t value	Conclusion
Enough	2.785	Significant

Table 71
Availability of Pure Water is Greater in Kalady Then That of Palakad

Test for proportion

Category	t value	Conclusion
Enough	4.722	Significant

Proportion of mills having the facilities is enough in Kalady is greater than that of Palakkad for analyzing by applying proportion test.

$$t = \sqrt{\frac{pq}{n}}$$ where

$$p_1 = \frac{x_1}{n_1} = \frac{\text{Number of respondent}}{\text{Total number of respondent}}$$

$$p_2 = \frac{x_2}{n_2} = \frac{\text{Number of respondent favoured pallakad}}{\text{Total number of respondent in palakad}}$$

$$P = 1 - q = \frac{x_1 + x_2}{n_1 + n_2} \text{ and } n = n_1 + n_2$$

Ho : $P_1 = P_2$
H1 : $P_1 > P_2$

Reject the null hypothesis when ever the calculated value is greater than the tabled value. In the case of Z and t the tabled value at the 5% per cent level (i.ep=.05) is 1.645.

The major findings can be summerised as follows:

- There is positive relationship between entrepreneurial growth and availability of pure water resulting in the clusteirng of rice mills in and around Kalady.
- Technical progress of modern rice mills bears a positive influence on sales.
- The growth of rice mill cluster in Kalady is rapid after 1980.
- Majority of rice mills (76per cent), find their investment for capital from Banks and other financial institutions.
- Of the 42 units surveyed only 36 per cent units are highly advanced and 14 per cent are advanced, 50 per cent are using moderate technology.
- There is not a single unit working on traditional lines in Kalady.
- Of the 42 units surveyed 71 per cent are newly started 19 per cent are converted into modern rice mills and 4 per cent are inherited.

- Majority of rice mills are operating on Partnership basis (67per cent), 19 per cent are working as sole proprietorship, and 14 per cent as private limited companies.
- There is neither government owned rice mills nor Co-operative sector rice mills working in Kalady.
- 79 per cent of the total units surveyed are working on 50-75 per cent capacity level.
- 40 per cent of the units have more than 50-60 tonnes capacity per day.
- 55 per cent of the entrepreneurs got primary education, only 15 per cent are graduated, 3 per cent are post-graduated.
- 65 per cent of the entrepreneurs are in the age group of 40-50 categories, 18 per cent are in the age group of above 50 categories and 17 per cent belongs to the younger age group of 30-40.
- 96 per cent of the entrepreneurs belongs to the local area (in and around Kalady), only 4 per cent are from with in the district.
- 93 per cent of the rice mills are operating in their own premises and 7 per cent in rented premises.
- 38 per cent rice mills employed up to 25 persons and 24 per cent in between 25-40 persons and only 3 per cent employed persons above 60.
- 50 per cent of the skilled workers belong to the local area and 50 per cent from outside the local area including outside the state.
- All the skilled workers (100 per cent) belong to the male category. Majority (55 per cent) of the un- skilled workers belong to the out side state.
- All the un skilled (100 per cent) workers are male workers.
- 88 per cent of the administrative staff belongs to the local area.

- 68 per cent of the administrative staff are graduated, 22 per cent are post graduated.
- 72 per cent of the administrative staff are males and 28 per cent are females.
- All the units are producing 'matta' variety rice.
- 93 per cent of the rice mills have their own storage facility and others have rented storage facility.
- 79 per cent of rice mills purchasing paddy on daily basis.
- Tamilnadu is the major supplier of paddy for the rice mills in Kalady.
- Karnataka ranks second in supplying paddy and Kerala has the sixth position in supplying paddy.
- Majority of rice mills (65 per cent) are making sales in Kerala only.
- The fast moving category is 10 Kg. packets.
- 32 units reported that they have joint- business activities.
- Kerala Rice Mill Owners Association is the only association working among the rice mill owners.
- The Paddy open Market Yard operated jointly by the rice mill owners association and the Kalady rice millers consortium is the biggest paddy open market in Kerala.
- Shimoga district in Karnataka ranks first in supplying paddy to the rice mills in Kalady among the other districts in the country.

CONCLUSION

In Kalady, the rice mill cluster is also having the availability of paddy from near by places and the abundant supply of pure water from the perennial water source of the river Periyar, and the entrepreneurial ability of the people in and around Kalady has contributed much to its growth. The use of 'Kalady Rice' a traditional brand name for best quality rice in large scale resulted the concentration and conglomeration of modern rice mill cluster in and around Kalady.

The growth of rice mill cluster was rapid after 1980s.the major market for the 'Kalady rice' is inside Kerala. Majority of sales (57%) are made through the retailers. Under Kalady rice millers consortium (KRMC) more than 39 mills have formed a private limited company with in the business for joint-business tie ups. In2004 the KRMC established a common facility expeller extraction unit, which helped the rice mills to convert their un- used by- products -rice bran as cooking, edible oil and to get good price. This is value addition and value creation and more over, it is a product innovation technique.

In Kalady rice mill cluster, there is only one association - the rice mill owners association - working on state as well as district basis, provides various services to its members. They advice its members in legal matters, form market strategies, solve trade union problems etc.This rice mill owners association has its own office space with a full-time secretary. The rice mill owners association also helps its members in financial matters too, i.e. providing a loan of up to Rs. 5lakhs in times of exigencies. This facility plays a critical role towards meeting un- foreseen exigencies of members. The rice mill cluster in Kalady found to be very significant role influencing and encouraging entrepreneurship.

The role of the Government of Kerala in developing the cluster seems to have been very significant. They provided with margin money loan of Rs.30lakh for the installation of the common facility centre expeller along with the consortium. This policy of the Government of Kerala is very encouraging. The other supporting agencies like Kerala Agricultural University, especially Rice Research Station, Pattambi. (RRS,Pattambi), Central Food technology Research Institute (CFTRI), Cochin University of Science And Technology (CUSAT), Pollution Control Board, District Industries Centre etc. played a significant role in developing rice mill cluster in and around Kalady.

5

Performance Andproblems of Rice Mills in Kalady

PERFORMANCE ANALYSIS OF RICE MILL SECTOR

This analysis is made up by various Ratios such as Profitability ratios, Liquidity ratios, Turn over Ratios, Capital structure ratios. This analysis is made from the trading and profit and loss a/c and Balance sheet of the20 modern rice mills for five financial Years from 2000-01to2004-2005.These 20 rice mills are selected on the basis of their market share for their products . These rice mills together contribute40% of the total market share of rice and rice products.

Performance Analysis with Selected Ratios

Profitability ratios: They are designed to high light the end results of business activities which is the sole criterion of the over all efficiency of a business unit. Profitability is an indication of efficiency with which operations of the business are carried on. Poor operational efficiency may indicate poor sales and hence poor profit. A lower profitability may arise profitability as it indicates the return. Bankers, Financial institutions, and creditors look at the profitability ratios as indicator whether or not the firm earns substantially more than it pays interest for the use of borrowed funds and whether ultimate repayment of their debt appears reasonably. Certain owners are interested to know the profitability as it indicates the return which they can get on their investments. The following are the profitability ratios.

$$\text{Gross profit ratio} = \frac{\text{Gross Profit}}{\text{Sales}} \times 100$$

Gp ratio increase due to increase in sales volume corresponding with decrease in cost of goods sold. Decrease in sales volume corresponding with increase in cost of goods sold shows less Gross profit.

Table 1
Average Gross Profit Ratio of 20 Modern Rice Mills for the Five Financial Years (2000-01 to 2004-05)

Rice mill No.	*GP ratio (%)*
1	9.93
2	8.32
3	9.89
4	9.68
5	8.37
6	10.42
7	7.75
8	9.08
9	8.81
10	5.24
11	11.65
12	11.51
13	24.80
14	7.45
15	3.61
16	9.30
17	9.14
18	9.40
19	7.65
20	10.27
Industrial Average	9.61

Rice mills No.10, 11 maintain comparatively higher rate of gross profit. It is to be noted that all the 20 modern rice mills have gross profit. In other words all the 20 modern rice mills have excess sales than the cost of sales.

All the 20 modern rice mills have gross profit. Rice mill No. 13 has the highest average gross profit and rice mill No. 15 has the lowest gross profit rate. The industrial average gross profit rate is 9.61%

Table 2
Average Net Profit of 20 Modern Rice Mills for the Five Financial Years (2000-01 to 2004-05)

Rice mill No.	*Net profit*	*Net profit ratio (%)*
1	828196	1.74
2	507488	0.51
3	577209	1.14
4	195723	0.21
5	573634	0.70
6	160004	0.15
7	339247	0.47
8	384415	0.48
9	906959	1.07
10	485121	0.45
11	469887	1.12
12	802493	1.49
13	426428	2.13
14	1002516	1.65
15	299211	0.70
16	366484	0.38
17	253777	0.34
18	155555	0.64
19	311345	0.93
20	547104	0.65
Industrial Average	469640	0.85

Making profit is the primary goal of any business firm. Profit is the excess of income over expenditure. Profit is the main motivator, strong sustainer, judicious allocator of resources, objective indicator of productivity and solid basis for growth, expansion and survival. In business profit is the prime incentive for an entrepreneur to produce what consumer wants. Profit is the inspiration for the businessman to innovate new products and new methods of production.

Net Profit Ratio

This ratio helps in determining the efficiency with which affairs of business are being managed. An increase in the ratio over previous period indicates improvement in the operational efficiency of the business provided the gross profit ratio is constant. Constant ratio in the above ratio year after year is a definite indication of improving conditions of the business

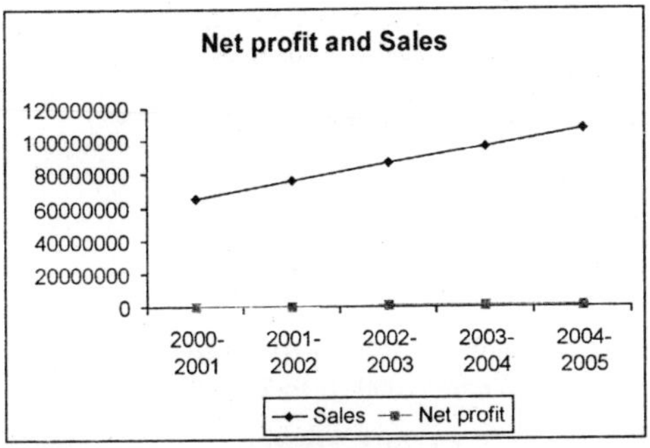

Figure 1

Table 2 shows the average net profit and percentage of average net profit for the five financial years. Rice mills No.3, 9, 11, 12, 13, and 14 are maintaining highest rate of net profit. Rice mills No.1, 2, 3, 5, 9, 12, 14, and 20 are maintaining highest amount of net profit than all other rice mills. The industrial average rate is 0.85% and an amount of Rs.469640. Only 8 modern rice mills have average net profit less than the industrial average. Rice mill No.14 has the highest amount of average net profit. (Rs. 10,2516)

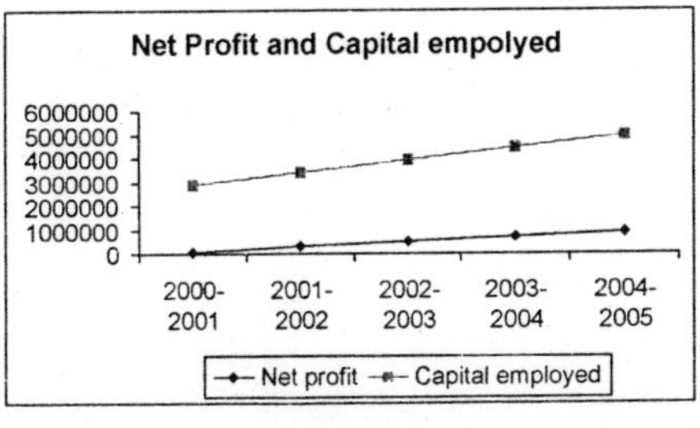

Figure 2

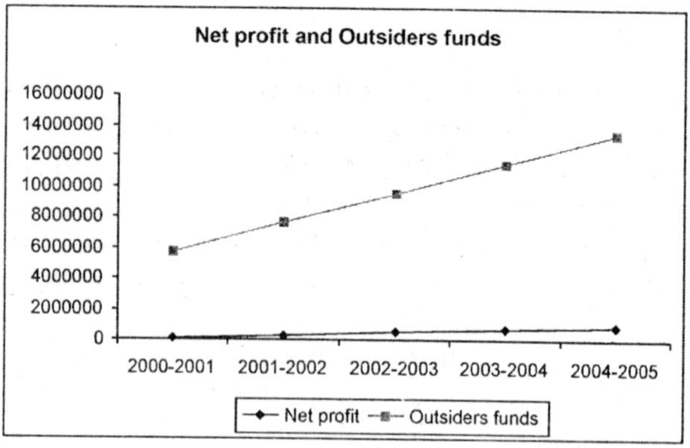

Figure 3

LIQUIDITY RATIOS

Table 3
Average Current Ratio of 20 Modern Rice Mills for the Five Financial Years (2000-01 to 2004-05)

$$\text{Current Ratio} = \frac{\text{Current Assets}}{\text{Current Liabilities}} \quad \text{suitable Ratio} = 2:1$$

Rice mill No.	*Current Ratio*
1	1.83:1
2	1.85:1
3	9.63:1
4	2.74:1
5	3.42:1
6	3.69:1
7	1.29:1
8	3.06:1
9	3.70:1
10	5.07:1
11	10.17:1
12	2.23:1
13	10.46:1
14	7.58:1
15	9.21:1
16	11.08:1
17	2.20:1
18	4.58:1
19	2.77:1
20	2.21:1
Industrial Average	4.12:1

Current assets are cash in hand, cash at bank, bills receivables, debtors, work in progress, stock, short -term marketable securities ,prepaid expenses etc. Current liabilities mean the liabilities repayable with in the same period i.e. a year, and generally include the following- sundry creditors, , bills payable, out standing expenses, taxes payable, bank overdraft, other liabilities payable with in a year.

Table 3 shows the average current ratio. The current ratio shows the relationship between current assets and current liabilities. Current ratio shows the ability to pay off its current liabilities. Its suitable (ideal) ratio is 2:1.In majority of the modern rice mills the current ratio is ideal or suitable. This shows the ability of the modern rice mills to meet its current liabilities. The industrial average is also highly suitable. Only 3 modern rice mills have below the suitable (ideal) ratio current assets and current liabilities. This ratio is also known as 'working capital ratio'. But this ratio is not sufficient to measure the adequacy or inadequacy of the working capital. A relatively high current ratio represented by the modern rice mills in and around Kalady showed that they are in a position to meet its current liabilities and there liquidity position is good. In the above table some of the rice mills showed an excessive ratio..It is generally observed that shows the in efficiency of the rice mills andit indicate over investment in working capital and improper utilisation of funds etc. Whether a ratio is excess or insufficient is determined by the particular circumstance of the business. In this business it is necessary to maintain comparatively higher ratio as its raw material (paddy) is available only in seasons of harvest. In this case the slow moving inventory constitutes the major share of the current assets, so the ratio of higher rate is suitable. In general, a current ratio of 2:1 is considered satisfactory. This is known as the 'rule of the thumb' or standard ratio. It requires that the current assets shall be twice the current liabilities. The purpose of fixing this standard is that liabilities should be met as and when they occur and there shall not be any difficulty in carrying on the normal operations. The size and nature of the business and the quality of assets are also material considerations in determine liquidity.

Table 4
Average Absolute Cash Position to Quickliabilites for the Five Financial Years (2000-01 to 2004-05)

Rice mill No.	*Cash Position*	*Quick liabilities*	*Absolute cash ratio*
1	140345	2120293	0.753
2	419367	6133831	0.0618
3	246081	2001797	0.3202
4	588560	9301283	0.0722
5	145133	3421749	0.0446
6	436697	1663000	0.4593
7	436522	7718829	0.0522
8	167680	1562323	0.1151
9	148996	3715722	0.0399
10	102506	1479488	0.0699
11	213440	2933569	0.0882
12	73057	4295701	0.0171
13	68160	916725	0.0889
14	36974	838939	0.0461
15	67865	817167	0.1750
16	82765	1539343	0.0638
17	97076	3236891	0.0300
18	67325	793264	0.1210
19	109408	1335386	0.0848
20	485789	5063923	0.0975
Industrial Average	206687	3044461	0.1061

$$\text{Absolute cash position ratio} = \frac{\text{Actual cash position}}{\text{Quick liabilities}}$$

Liquidity of a business can be viewed from an extremely conservative point of view and the absolute cash position can be measured through this method- absolute cash ratio. But this ratio is not very popular with the analysts. It is revealed that all the rice mills are maintaining cash reserve to meet the daily needs. Majority of the units are maintaining only limited cash reserve but only few units are maintaining good cash reserve. The nature of the business is one of the factors that determine the cash requirement. In the rice mill business raw material are available in seasons it requires to maintain reasonable cash reserve. Total cash position and the quick liabilities are the two factors or constituents in this ratio. From the current assets items of inventory, prepaid expenses etc. are subtracted and from the current liabilities bank overdraft is deducted. The industrial average is also showed a small cash position as the majority of the transactions are credit based.

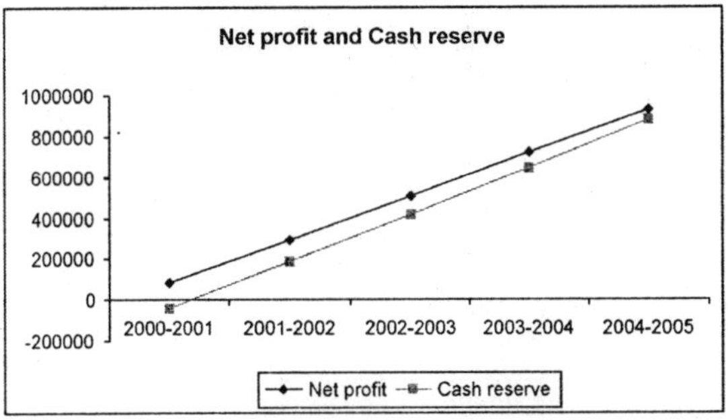

Figure 4

Solvency Ratios (Capital Structure Ratios)

Table 5 shows the debt equity position of the 20 modern rice mills in and around Kalady.Gearing ratio shows the relationship of long-term debt to total capital is considered the most important by many investors and financial analysts. Popularly known as debt- equity ratio, this ratio has utility to many including share holders (Proprietors), creditors, suppliers and other user groups. Long term creditors are interested to in knowing whether the capital structure of the company represents financial burden on them or not. The overall sound financial position depends up on sound liquidity as well as solvency position. They are interested in two things;

1. Sufficient margin of safety for their lending's;
2. Adequacy of profits of the company to pay interest charges and installments of the principal amount, if any becoming due.

For analysis they rely upon ratios which are usually called leverage or capital structure ratios e.g. debt-equity ratio. Leverage ratios may be calculated from the balance sheet items to determine the proportion of debt in total financing. The

Table 5
Average Debt Equity Ratio of Five Financial Years (2000-01 to 2004-05)

Rice mill No.	*Outsiders funds*	*Capital employed*	*Debt-equity ratio*
1	2575707	2176550	1.18:1
2	9534841	3918998	2.43:1
3	5116587	6795241	0.75:1
4	8890147	7321497	1.21:1
5	11224170	5350707	2.10:1
6	20636023	14081467	1.47:1
7	13272651	1380084	9.62:1
8	8507534	1645192	5.17:1
9	16104069	1117392	14.41:1
10	11843650	861574	13.75:1
11	10237097	2448904	4.18:1
12	7463786	2426580	3.08:1
13	1933770	512113	3.78:1
14	8017711	1101549	7.28:1
15	6569316	899902	7.30:1
16	35243586	1944915	18.12:1
17	8725764	1804585	4.84:1
18	3416639	1007460	3.39:1
19	3609690	1269792	2.84:1
20	9963256	3997530	2.49:1
Industrial Average	10144300	3103101	3.27:1

Source: Audited Financial Statements of Modern rice mills.

fundamental objective of computing this ratio is to measure the relative interest of owners and creditors. The most important ratio for determining the solvency position is 'debt-equity ratio'.

Debt –equity ratio

$$= \frac{\text{Loan capital} + \text{preference share capital}}{\text{Capital employed (net tan gible assets)}}$$

$$\text{Debt to equity ratio} = \frac{\text{External equities}}{\text{Internal equities}}$$

$$\text{Or Debt to equity ratio} = \frac{\text{Outsiders funds}}{\text{Share holders funds}}$$

Net tangible asset (Capital employed) is obtained by subtracting the intangible assets and the current assets from total assets. Loan capital plus preference capital constitute the amount of long–term debt. It is said that as a rule or thumb, one should not opt for a company whose long –term debt exceeds two–thirds of its total capitalisation.In this case majority of rice mills are running at a dangerous position as the borrowed funds are more than two third of its total capital. A company or business depending on large amounts of debt should manage and perform well to avoid any worse contingencies. Debt –equity ratios should be analysed not for one but for many years to determine a trend .In this case the long term debt is increasing than the capital employed, there is a danger position prevailing in the whole rice mill sector but the demand and supply position of this business is very favourable as the demand is more than the supply. The underlying idea of calculating debt- equity ratio is to measure the relative interest of the creditors and owners. It indicates to the extend to which debt financing has been used in the business. It shows the creditors the extend of their interest being covered by the net worth of the company. A high debt to equity ratio is generally considered unfavourable.In such a case 'margin of safety' for creditors will be less. But during prosperity period alow debt to equity is unfavourable to the proprietors or share holders because cost of debt being less "trading on equity" will increase return for the owners of the business.

But this business can able to earn a return on the assets higher than the rate of interest on long term debt; the enterprise makes an over-all profit. But if the enterprise runs risk of not earning a return on assets equal to the interest cost of the long term debt , the enterprise makes an over all loss. But in the case of modern rice mill business every unit is running at a profit and making a profit more than to pay off its long term interest coverage. The industrial average of long term debt and capital employed also shows a high gearing. This shows the sign of over gearing and this trend should be discouraged for the years to come. A firm with higher proportion of external debt in its capital structure is more risky compared to a firm with a comparatively lower proportion of external debt. The firm with higher proportion of external debt has fixed commitment to pay interest and to repay principal amount and this can be encouraged during 'Boom' periods.

TURNOVER RATIOS

The working capital of a business is the excess of current assets over current liabilities; this is computed by subtracting current liabilities from the current assets.

Working capital = Current Assets - Current Liabilities

This ratio reveals the use of working capital for the effective functioning of the rice mill business. In other words working capital is the amount required for the day to day operations of the business. Here the 'Funds' are effectively utilised for the proper functioning of the business.

The industrial average of the working capital turnover is 22.30. The Working capital turnover is calculated by =Net Sales. In rice mill No. 1 shows the highest turnover ratio as the sales are very high when compared to the working capital. In Rice mill No. 7 also the turnover ratios are very high than the industrial average.

Table 6
Average Working Capital Turnover Ratios for the Five Financial Years (2000-01 to 2004-05)

Rice mill No.	*Working Capital turnover ratios*
1	73.16
2	18.61
3	11.31
4	14.22
5	23.51
6	4.81
7	80.88
8	28.03
9	39.00
10	18.50
11	6.24
12	8.61
13	18.34
14	12.27
15	14.51
16	7.21
17	20.65
18	13.54
19	15.22
20	17.36
Industrial Average	22.30

Source: Audited Financial Statements

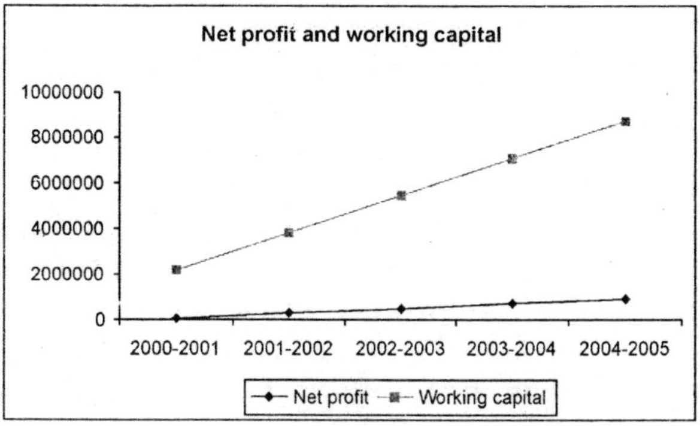

Figure 5

Table 7
Average Fixed Assets Turnover ratios for the Five Financial Years (2000-01 to 2004-05)

Rice Mill No.	*Average Fixed Assets turnover Ratios*
1	12.94
2	11.16
3	11.38
4	11.41
5	11.82
6	9.03
7	42.55
8	11.65
9	25.19
10	14.98
11	10.13
12	8.84
13	11.54
14	16.98
15	10.73
16	16.22
17	10.82
18	11.76
19	5.59
20	10.58
Industrial Average	13.77

Source: Audited Financial Statements.

Fixed assets turnover ratio is calculated by establishing the relationship between sales or cost of sales.

$$\text{Fixed assets turnover ratio} = \frac{\text{Net sales}}{\text{Fixed assets}}$$

The ratio gives an idea about adequate investment, over investment or under investment in fixed assets. As a rule or thumb, over investment in unprofitable fixed assets should be avoided to the possible extent; under investment is also equally bad affecting unfavourably the operating costs and consequently the profit. This ratio assumes added significance in the case of manufacturing business like rice mills. An increase in the ratio is an indicator of efficiency of the business. A decrease in the ratio reveals of un-wise and improper investment in fixed assets. Here the industrial average as wellas the individual ratios shows the efficiency of the rice mill business that the fixed assets are fruitfully utilised.

Table 8
Average Total Assets Turnover Ratio of the Five Financial Years (2000-01 to 2004-05)

Rice mill No.	*Average total assets turnover ratio*
1	6.92
2	4.53
3	4.02
4	3.53
5	5.16
6	2.87
7	15.87
8	7.00
9	10.48
10	6.18
11	3.51
12	2.97
13	3.03
14	5.88
15	5.46
16	4.43
17	5.37
18	5.90
19	3.50
20	4.52
Industrial Average	5.52

Source : Audited Financial Statements

This ratio shows the relationship between total assets of the business and sales. The total assets are taken at the value shown at the end of the year as a whole. Total Assets Turnover ratio; this ratio shows the efficiency of assets management. This ratio indicates the utilisation of total assets in the operation of the concern. It is used to judge the effectiveness of the use of the total assets and to study the trend of over- investment in assets or otherwise. All the rice mills in and around Kalady are properly utilising the total assets .The assets are effectively and fruitfully utilised for making sales and earning net profits.

Hypothesis No. 4

The debt- equity ratio of technically advanced mills (Fully - Automated) are found to be low as per the analysis. The hypothesis formulated to test the relationship is: Technically progressed mills have lesser debt-equity ratio. The test reuslts are given in the Table 12 The Z test applied confirms the relationship.

Table 9

Technically Progressed Mills have lesser Debit Equity Ratio

Advancement	*Mean*	*Std.Deviation*	*CV*	*Z*	*Conclusion*
Sales Highly Advanced	9.8282	16.66580	169.57	1.703	Significant
Sales Advanced	5.2567	0. 90360	188.40		

The long-term borrowing and capital are effectively invested in fixed assets and working capital (net current assets) of the rice mills business. The detailed examination of the financial structure of the 20 modern rice mills for a period of five years substantiated that capital employed and long-term borrowing (outsiders fund) are effectively and fruitfully invested in fixed assets and working capital (Hypothesis No. 5). Test results are shown in Table 10.

Table 10 shows long term borrowings (outsdiers funds) and capital are effectively invested in fixed assets and working capital (current assets) of all the 20 modern rice mills.

Rice is a major food crop of Kerala and majority of farmers are rice farmers. The prosperity of the people of Kerala is based on the performance of rice crop and hence Kerala's economy is rice based. Rice is cultivated through out Kerala. Rice crop is cultivated in a diversity of conditions and probably no where else the crop is cultivated under such situations.

Table 10

		Capital employed	*Outsiders funds*
Capital employed	Pearson Correlation	1	.145
	Sig. (2-tailed)		.150
	N	100	100
Fixed assets	Pearson Correlation	.586(**)	.282(**)
	Sig. (2-tailed)	.000	.005
	N	100	100
Outsiders funds	Pearson Correlation	.145	1
	Sig. (2-tailed)	.150	
	N	100	100
Total assets	Pearson Correlation	.114	.151
	Sig. (2-tailed)	.259	.135
	N	100	100
Working capital	Pearson Correlation	.630(**)	.314(**)
	Sig. (2-tailed)	.000	.001
	N	100	100

** 1% level significance.

The area and production of rice during 1970 were increasing but from 1980 onwards it showed a declining trend. The gap between demand and supply of rice which was 50per cent till the mid seventies, started widening there after consistent to the large scale shift in paddy lands for cultivation of other more remunerative crops like coconut, rubber, banana etc.This area and production of rice succumb to economic pressure emanating from the remunerative crops. There was a decline of more than 5 lakh ha of area under paddy cultivation during the last two decades. The twenty five year period from mid-seventies witnessed large scale shift in area under the crop. Rice production touched it peak level of around 14 lakh million tonnes in mid seventies with a coverage of 8.81 lakh ha. The gap in meeting the internal demand of food grains was estimated to be 50 per cent during the period.

Socio-economic-ecological impacts of paddy field conversion are the central theme of political, economic debate in Kerala. From the socio-economic point of view , the production of rice the staple food of Keralites which forms about 90 per cent of food grains cultivated in the state , is in adequate to meet the ever increasing demand for rice from inside the state it self. The valuable service provided by the paddy field should also be considered along with the monitory and fiscal loss by conservation of paddy fields

Table 11
Area Under Rice Cultivation

Year	*Area (ha)*
1974-75	8.8 lakhs
1984-85	7.3 lakhs
1994-95	5.3 lakhs
2003-04	2.87 lakh

During the same period the share of coconut in the total cropped area has increased from 21.3 per cent to 35.06 per cent, rubber increased from 5.2 per cent to 18.41 per cent. Other cash crops such as banana, cashew nut etc have also improved their share in the total cropped area at the expense of rice. The rice mills in Kerala are in a disadvantageous position, since the production of raw materials is in adequate to meet its requirement Hypo thesis test No. 1.

The deceleration in production of rice is due to the negative change in cropping pattern effect in the state of Kerala. (Alternative Hypothesis (H_1).

Null Hypothesis (H_0): There is no relationship between production and cropping pattern effect.

METHODOLOGY

Type and source of data: The main source of data for this analysis is from various issues of Economic review and Statistical Abstract published by Government of Kerala. The data used for this analysis are the state level out put, yield, area and harvest prices of paddy in the year 1994-95. The prices of 1994-95 are taken as the base year.

The study has been done for the time period of 1974-75 to 2003-04. In Kerala the production of rice was much higher in the year 1974-75.This is why the present study began from the year 1974-75. The study ended 2003-04 since at the time of data collection the data were available up to 2003-04.

Decomposition of out put growth is not a new concept in the field of agriculture growth analysis. Still it has its usual importance to the researchers and policy makers for identifying the root causes of high and low growth of agricultural output. Although some attempts were made earlier to explain agricultural growth under additive schemes, the first systematic study came from Minhas and Vaidynathan (1965). Even though there are different models and concepts of growth decomposition under additive scheme and multiplicative scheme where additive scheme are used to decompose the absolute growth rate and for relative growth decomposition multiplicative schemes are used. Minhas and Vaidynathan used additive scheme model.

Model measurers the contribution of area, yield and cropping pattern respectively in the absolute change in the value of gross agricultural output. Model is of the form

$$Q_t - Q_o = (A_t - A_0)\, S\, W_i C_{io} Y_{io} + A_t S\, W_i C_{io}(Y_{it} - Y_{io}) + A_t S\, W_i Y_{io}$$
$$(C_{it} - C_{io}) + A_t S\, wi\, (Y_{it} - Y_{io})(C_{it} - C_{io})$$

Where Q_t, A_t, Y_{it} are respectively the values of output , gross cropped area, cropping pattern , yield at time t and wi is the constant price weight. The last term shows the interaction effect of yield and cropping pattern change. A positive interaction would imply that the crop structure has shifted in favour of those crops which show higher growth yield. The pure cropping pattern effect if positive would show a shift in favour of high initial productivity crops.

Another important contribution of to the Minhas – Vaidynathan scheme was the introduction of another crop structural component viz.the locational component.

Dharamnarain decomposed component of productivity as pure effect of yield, locational and cropping pattern and interaction due to cropping pattern and other locational effect. A positive locational component indicates a shift in crop location from low productivity region to high productivity region.

MODEL FOR DECOMPOSITION

All decomposition models used in the Kerala agriculture consist of interaction terms. InDharamnarains model also there was two interactions-cropping interaction and location interaction. Decomposition without an interaction term is the first attempt in Kerala agriculture the decomposition model with the interaction term has certain disadvantages as it either under estimates or over estimates the pure effect of the variable. In the multiplicative frame work, consistent decomposition model with out any interaction term has been introduced for the first time by JamalAzad (1992) but no such attempt has been made in the additive frame work. Consistent decomposition of out put growth with the appropriate additive model with out any interaction term is put forward by Majumdar and Basu (2005).

For this study additive model with out interaction term is used. At the constant price weight the value of out put can broadly be decomposed in two components (1) area and (2) productivity. Again productivity consists of two items (1) yield and (2) cropping pattern or inter-crop allocation. In the case of individual crop there is no difference between yield and productivity. So ultimately the components of growth considered for output decomposition in the present study are area, yield and cropping pattern. In general explanations of the area component takes into account rate of growth of gross cropped area that includes the impact of change both in the net sown area and cropping intensity. The yield component measurers the impact of change in output per hectare. Cropping pattern change implies to what extent area is shifted from a low yield crop to a highly yield crop.

As mentioned above, the three components area, yield and cropping pattern have been considered in the present study for output decomposition. The effect of each component is evaluated using as weights, different combinations of base and terminal years values of other two components. In fact for this crop the effect weight is the arithmetic mean of three items. The first two items represent the base year and terminal year values of the products of the remaining components and third item is the average of the products obtained by alternatively taking base year and terminal year values of the other remaining component.

Output Growth

Area effect | Yield Effect | Cropping Pattern Effect

$$\text{Output growth} = A_t S W_i C_{it} Y_{it} - A_o S W_i C_{io} Y_{io}$$

$$A.E = {}^1/_3 [(A_t - A_o) \{SW_i C_{io} Y_{io} + S W_i C_{io} Y_{it} + {}^1/_2 (S W_i C_{io} Y_{it} + S W_i C_{it} Y_{io})\}]$$

$$Y.E = {}^1/_3 A_o S W_i (Y_{it} - Y_{io}) C_{io} + {}^1/_3 A_t SW_i (Y_{it} - Y_{io}) C_{it} + {}^1/_6 A_o S W_i (Y_{it} - Y_{io}) C_{it} + {}^1/_6 A_t SW^1 (Y_{it} - Y_{io}) C_{io}$$

$$C.P.E = {}^1/_3 A_o S W_i (C_{it} - C_{io}) Y_{io} + {}^1/_3 A_t SW_i (C_{it} - C_{io}) Y_{it} + {}^1/_6 Ao S W_i (C_{IT} - C_{io}) Y_{it} + {}^1/_6 A_t S W_i (C_{it} - C_{io}) Y_{io}$$

The variables and notations used in the model are :

$At = Sa_{it}$ = Gross Cropped Area where ai is the area under ith crop.

$Yit = V_{it}/A_t$ = yield of the ith crop

$Cit = A_{it}/A_t$ = Share of the ith crop in gross cropped area all at time t.

W=Constant price weight.

The subscripts '0" and 't' refer respectively to the base and 't' the peirod. Subscript 'i' is used for the ith crop.

In output decomposition, under linear framework, the effect of each component (yield, area, cropping pattern) measures output growht due to that particular component. For example, yield effect indicates the output growht due to growht in yield.

DECOMPOSITION ANALYSIS

Total Out put growth decomposed in to three effects using the formula.

$$\text{Output Growth} = A + SW_i C_i + Y_{it} - Ao\ SW_i C_{io} Y_{io}$$

The effects are computed by its formula.

Three Effects : Area Effect, Yield Effect and Cropping Pattern effect.

Output growth= Area Effect+ Yield Effect + Cropping Pattern Effect

In Period I: (1974-75to 1980-81) positive output growth obtained due to the impact of cropping pattern effect. Contribution of are effect and yield effect are negative.

In Period II: (1980-81 to 1991-92) significant positive output growth is the contribution of cropping pattern only. Negative output growth is in the period II signifies the deteriorating tendency of output growth. Output growth of the crop rice is decreasing due to the effect of cropping pattern where the share of rice to the total cropped area is decreasing from period I to Period III. Growth rates also show the negative trend in output growth only the yield effect growth rates show the positive values.

Table 12
Absolute Output Growth
Base Year is T.E 1994-95.

Rice	*Period I (1974-75 to1980-81)*	*Period II (1980-81) to1991-92)*	*Period III (1992-93) to 2003-04)*	*I*	*II*	*III*
Out put growth	(-.59)	*(-.67)	**(-.96)		R^2= 46 DW = 1.76	R^2= 93 DW=1.175
Area effect	**(-.93)	(.87)	(-.55)	R^2= 87 DW-1.63	R^2= .76	
Yield Effect	*(.77)	**(.88)	*(.65)	R^2-.59 DW 2.192	R^2= .77 DW^2=2.3	R^2= .43 DW=1.55
Cropping Pattern effect	**(-.91)	**(-.99)	(-.98)	R^2=.83 DW=2.416	R^2=.98 DW^2=1.344	

*5% level significance (Grwoth Rates) **1% level of significance (Percentage contribution).

Growth Rates Computed by Regression Method (OLS)

Tendency of output growth before and after the bench mark year shows the declining nature of out put growth. Value of Absolute area effect remains negative before and after the base year shows the stable nature, Yield effect changes from negative to positive signifies the increasing nature and value of cropping effect changes from positive to negative shows the declining of the effect. The deterioration in area of cultivation and production of rice is due to the negative impact of cropping pattern effect. This is tested using the hypothesis deceleration in production of rice is due to the negative change in cropping patter in the state of Kerala. (Alternative Hypothesis - H_1). The null hypothesis (H_0) is that there is no relationship between production and cropping pattern effect.

The test results (Table 12) confirms the alternative hypothesis and rejects the null hypothesis. The deceleration in production of rice is due to the negative change in cropping pattern in the state of Kerala. (Alternative Hypothesis- (H_1). The Null Hypothesis (H_0) is that there is no relationship between production and cropping pattern effect. The null hypothesis is rejected and alternative hypothesis is accepted.

PROBLEMS OF RICE MILLS IN AND AROUND KALADY

Table 13

Ranking of the Problems Faced by the Rice Mill cluster in Kalady

Problems	*Weighted Score*	*Percentage to total*	*Rank*
Shortage of raw material	279	15.5	I
Cost of electricity, transportation cost	202	11.2	II
High Cost of input	176	9.8	III
High cost of packing materials	157	8.7	IV
Inadequate price for by-products	124	6.9	V
Improper Utilisation of Husk	117	6.5	VI
Un healthy competition	113	6.3	VII
Problem of storage facilities	112	6.2	VIII
Unorganized markeitng net work	108	6.0	IX
Poor linkage with supporting industries	106	5.9	X
High quantity of effluent	104	5.8	X1
High Advertisemnet cost	103	5.7	X11
Unstable selling price of rice	99	5.5	XIII
Aggregate weighted score	1800	100	

Shortage of Raw Material

The main and the only raw material for rice processing is paddy. The process of boiling, drying and milling of paddy will convert it into rice, rice bran and husk. Rice is the main product, bran and husk are by-products. Rice is the major food crop of Kerala and the majority of farmers in the state are rice farmers. The area and production of rice was steadily increasing till the mid seventies had succumbed to economic pressure emanating from remunerative crops like coconut, rubber and banana. The urbanization which leads to the construction of the new generation schools and colleges , roads , houses etc.This all resulted in the decline of more than 5 lakh ha of area under paddy cultivation and consequently the production of paddy and rice . From the socio economic point of view , the production of paddy the staple food of 'Keralites' , which forms about 90 per cent of the food grains cultivated in the state , is inadequate to meet the demand for rice from with in the state of kerala.Due to the non-availability of paddy from Kerala , the rice mills in the has to depend up on other states like Tamilnadu, Karnataka, Maharastra,Andhrapradesh and even the North Indian states .Due to the heavy transportation cost , the cost of production increases and finally the product cost and the selling price. The paddy from the North Indian states is transported to Kalady through Rail ways. The commission agents, transporting agents etc are the middlemen in the rice trade. There is no facility to collect paddy from farmers of Karnataka, Tamilnadu, and Andhra Pradesh and from the North Indian states and thereby availability of consistent quality raw paddy is not assured. There is no facility for testing moisture content, immature paddy content and contamination of other foreign materials in the paddy. In the rice mill business quality of raw paddy is considered to be the most important deciding factor of rice quality.

Now with the joint- activities of Kalady Rice Millers Consortium (KRMC) and Kerala Rice Mill Owners Association, a common paddy market yard is established at Kalady.About 120 truck loads of paddy carrying 10metric a tonne of paddypertruck (1200MT) from different parts of the country is arriving on an average. The development of this open market yard can reduce the problem of raw material shortage to a certain extent in future. But if the processing industries are started in these states on a large-scale, the problem of raw material shortage is a serious threat to the rice mill cluster in and around Kalady.

Cost of Electricity, Transportation Cost and Fuel Charges

The total power requirement of each unit is approximately 160HP which is supplying through LTconnection. One of the serious problems faced by the Modern rice mills are the highest power tariff levied by the KeralaState Electricity Board (KSEB) for the power consumption. For drying the parboiled rice in drier un- interrupted power supply is required .Failure of power supply is a common feature that creates damage and loss to the modern rice mills. As an alternative for this all the modern rice mills in and around Kalady have installed their own diesel generators which also resulted increase in the cost of production. The increasing trend of fuel charges is a serious problem faced by the modern rice mills in and around Kalady. The occasional power cut imposed by the government also increases the cost of production of this food processing units. Another important problem is the cost of transportation. Due to the non- availability or shortage of paddy with in the state the modern rice mills have to depend other states for their paddy requirement which resulted in heavy ransportation costs. Un-reasonable and un –timely hike in fuel charges create problems to this processing units.

High Cost of Inputs

One and only raw material for this industry is paddy.Nowa days the seasonal price fluctuation of the paddy is very high. In Kerala the production of paddy is deteriorated steadily year by year. The modern rice mill cluster in Kalady has to procure paddy regularly from other states. While procuring paddy individually by the modern rice mill units they could not enjoy the benefits of bulkpurchase. So this cluster requires bulk raw material purchase scheme so that they can enjoy the benefits of bulk purchase, bulk transportation, direct purchase from sources avoiding the middlemen etc.

Highcost of Packing Materials

Modern rice mill require packing materials such as jute and polythene bags in bulk. Now the modern rice mill units are individually purchasing these items at higher cost. This also increases the cost of rice. Jute bags are purchasing from the supporting jute bag industrial units and polythene bags are purchasing mainly from Coimbatore industrial area.

Inadequate Price for Rice Bran and Other By-products

Rice bran is the main byproduct of the rice processing units. Modern rice mills in and around Kalady alone produces 300MT of rice bran per day. Even though the commercial value of rice bran is very high, the rice mill units do not get the adequate price for their by-products. Rice bran is a highly sensitive products and quality deteriorate while storing. High quality rice bran oil is extracted only from fresh bran. The oil in bran contains some Free Fatty acids (FFA). The enzymatic hydrolysis goes on storing them and leads to rancidity. To avoid this bran is made to process with in 2 or 3 days from their production.

In Kerala only Two rice bran oil extraction units are functioning now. Most of the extraction units are functioning in Karnataka. So this rice bran is sold only through middle men. So the modern rice mill units do not get reasonable price for their main by product.

Improper Utilization Husk

The cost of electricity and fuel charges for operating is increasing on the one hand but there is no proper utilization of the husk from the modern rice mill. The average connected load of each unit is 160HP, and the cost of electricity is increasing steadily every year. The power generator system i.e. husk-fired boiler is not properly utilized and the fuel cost increases.

Unhealthy Competition

After 1990, a number of modern rice mill units established and these mills were located in Aluva, Kunnathunadu taluks of Ernakulam district. In a nut shell, these mills were mainly concentrated in and around Kalady, it creates unhealthy completion among the rice mill owners causes damage to the good will of many modern rice mills. Cut-throat competition of marketing products led to un healthy practices.

Problem of Storage Facilities

The modern rice mill cluster in Kalady require 300 lorry loads of paddy per day and the inflow from other states like Tamilnadu, Karnataka, etc. are seasonal The mill owners have to store huge quantities of paddy for the processing of rice. Each unit in the sector suffers from sufficient storage facility to store bulk quantities of paddy. The by products from the processing of rice is also to be stored other wise it will loss its value.

Un-organised Marketing Network

As the rice is produced in and around Kalady , the consumers are scattered in different parts of the country and abroad. Under this circumstance, the producer will not be able to sell the products to the ultimate consumers directly. The modern rice mills have to maintain a very large sale force, separate outlets, problem of management and control etc. need huge investment of financial resources. So in order to avoid, this many modern rice mills depend intermediaries to market their product, this in turn creates additional cost.

Poor Linkage with Supporting Industries

Forward linkage and backward linkage with the supporting industries is not at all satisfactory. Linkage with the by- product receiving and supplying units will definitely increase the profit margin of the modern rice mills and also the supporting industries. Linkage with paddy supplying units, packing material units, power supply units, by-product utilisation units are highly necessary.

High Quantity of Effluent

The paddy is parboiled with water for 6 hours. After 6 hours this water is drained out from the soaking tank of parboiling unit. This water is the main source of waste water. About 600 liters of is generated while processing 1 metric tonne of rawpaddy. The waste water contains suspend able solids, BODetc. The average processing capacity of modern rice mill is 40 metric tonnes of paddy per day.

So each unit produces 2500 liters of waste water per day. The Kerala State Pollution Control Board strictly insisted the units for construction of Effluent Treatment Plant (ETP) which requires huge investment of capital. Another effluent is the fly ash generated as a result of burning boiler.

High Advertisement Cost

Un-healthy and excess competition led the modern rice mills to advertise their product in market. To increase the sales it becomes a necessary to advertise the product both in print media and electronic media. Now a day the media advertisement is very costly and no unit can sustain with out advertisement. The consumers prefer to buy products on the basis of quality and bran name. Therefore to attract consumers a heavy amount must be spend by the modern rice mill units.

Un-stable Selling Price of Rice

The distributors, wholesalers and retailers in and out side the state is marketing the majority of rice and rice products. Only few units are exporting their products directly and a few through merchant exporters. Majority of the rice mill units in and around Kalady are selling their products with in the state. The catering units, Hotels and restaurants purchase the parboiled rice directly from the modern rice mill units. Due to the severe competition from the neighbouring states such as Andhra Pradesh, Tamilnadu etc, the price of rice is fluctuating un- reasonably and the modern rice mills in and around Kalady can't compete with them.

The Strength of Rice Mill Cluster in Kalady are

1. Availability of pure water from the perennial water source of river Periyar.
2. Management with good business back ground.
3. Proximity to paddy open market yard at Kalady.
4. Availability of good transport facilities.
5. Availability of Labour.
6. Availability of financial assistance.

7. Presence of strong and active association among the entrepreneurs.
8. Formation of Kerala rice miller's consortium (KRMC) for join-business tie–ups.

The Weaknesses of the Rice Mill Cluster in Kalady are

1. Non-consistent price of paddy.
2. Unseasoned scarcity of raw paddy.
3. High quantity of effluent.
4. Unstable selling price of rice.
5. Lack of knowledge in quality standards.
6. Lack of quality consistency in products.
7. Unhealthy competition.
8. Unorganised marketing net work.
9. Non-ability to market by products.
10. Poor linkage with supporting industries.

The Opportunities of the Rice Mill Cluster in Kalady are

1. Growing market as staple food of mankind.
2. Increase in population.
3. Development of High Yield Varieties of paddy seeds.
4. Cultivation of un-tapped areas in other parts of India and Kerala.
5. Application of by- products for various purposes.
6. Evolution of new technology for making value added products.
7. Absence of government restrictions.
8. Incentives from government for food processing industries.
9. Un-tapped export market.

The Threats of the Rice Mill Cluster in Kalady are

1. Stiff competition expected from countries like China, Pakistan, Thailand, Bangladesh, Cambodia, Korea, Taiwan and Philippines.

2. Change in negative cropping pattern effects i.e. cultivating remunerative crops other than paddy (rice)
3. Changing food habits of man kind.
4. Health problems related to diabetics, etc, that restrict the use of rice as staple food.

The Major Findings are the Following

1. The deceleration in production of Rice is due to the negative change in cropping pattern effect in the state of Kerala.
2. Technically progressed mills (fully Automated) have lesser debt-equity ratio that the technically less progressed mills (semi-Automated)
3. The long term borrowing and capital are effectively industries in fixed assets and working capital. (Current Assets) of the Rice mills.
4. All the 20 modern rice mills have net profit in the all the five financial years.
5. All the 20 modern rice mills showed gross profit.
6. All the 20 modern rice mills have cash reserve to meet exigencies.

CONCLUSION

Analysing performance of rice mills in and around Kalady in terms of output, finance and managerial aspects the following conclusions arrived. The mainfood of Kerala-rice-the area of cultivation and production is decreasing year by year due to the negative change incropping pattern effect i.e there is a shift in paddy lands for cultivation of other remunerative crops likes coconut, rubber banana etc. This is a serious threat to the rice processing mills, because paddy is the only raw material for this industry. While analysing the reasons for the clustering of rice mills in and around Kalady, - there are certain locational factors-the entrepreneurial growth and availability of pure water from the river Periyar are the reasons for the conglomeration of rice mills. All the 20 rice mills are running at a profit. The highly advanced (Fully automated) mills have an edge over technically less advanced (semi automated) mills in terms of sales. The debt equity ratio of the technically advanced mills are lesser than the less advance mills. (Semi Automated). All this 20 Rice mills are running at a high gearing in terms of capital structure.

6

SUMMARY AND CONCLUSION

Among the agro-industries, rice processing industry is the biggest industry in India. Rice is one of the important agricultural commodities .It is obtained by processing paddy. In Kerala rice is the staple food. Paddy processing industries are one of the traditional industries in Kerala. So an attempt has been made to study about the growth and development of rice trading in Kerala-especially in and around Kalady where more than 43 per cent of the modern rice mills are located.

The study is presented in six chapters. The first chapter is introduction which explain the conceptual frame work, importance of the study, review of the earlier studies, theoretical frame work, objectives, hypothesis, methodology, data source, limitations and design of the study.

Two types of data have been used in this study:

1. Primary data
2. Secondary data

The primary data for the study were collected from the rice traders, Rice mill owners association, Kalady rice miller's consortium (KRMC) field survey among 42 rice mill units, marginfreeshops etc. Data collected from employees of rice mills, brokers and commission agents, by the interview method. The selections of respondents were based on 42 modern rice mills in and around Kalady out of 80 mills in

Ernakulam district. Only 120 units are functioning in the state of Kerala. The sample units percentage is 35 per cent of the total modern rice mills in the state of Kerala and 52.5 per cent in Ernakulam District. 20 modern rice mills functioning in and around Kalady are selected for financial performance analysis on the basis of their market share in rice trading in the state of Kerala.This totals 16.6 per cent of the total rice mills in the state and 25 per cent of the total rice mills in Ernakulam district. Audited financial statements (Trading and Profit and loss account and Balance Sheet) were used from 2000-01 to 2004-05 (5 years), being the latest year in which data collection was possible.

The second Chapter deals with the Area, Production and Productivity of rice in India, Kerala, and Ernakulam district. As the rice is the major food crop of Kerala and majority farmers in the state are rice farmers. The prosperity of people of Kerala based on the performance of the rice crop and hence Kerala's economy is largely rice based. The area and production of rice which was steadily increasing till mid seventies had succumb to economic pressure emanating from other remunerative crops, and the growth of the construction sector. This resulted in the decline of more than 5 lakh ha of area under paddy cultivation during the last two decades. Socio-economic-ecological impacts of paddy field conversion are the central theme of this chapter.

Chapter 3 presents a historical sketch of the rice mill business in Kerala and Kalady. Different methods of rice processing and the conversion of by- products. Chapter -4 gives a detailed study of rice mill cluster in and around Kalady based on the Porters Diamond model of clustering. Chapter -5 presents a detailed analysis of the financial performance and problems of 20 selected modern rice mills having their own brand names for marketing their products and constitutes 40 per cent of the total market share in rice trading . Chapter -6 contains the findings, conclusions and interpretation of the results. Also suggestions for improvement of the industries and an enquiry into the possibility of further research in this area had been made.

FINDINGS

Specific finding in conformity with the objectives laid down are given below:

In Kerala, Rice is the Staple Food

Its food requriements are increasing year by year. But the production of rice is deteriorated year by year due to the negative impact of cropping pattern change. In Kerala, mid seventies were a period of highest area of paddy cultivaiton and production. But after that period, the rice production and are aof cultivaiton succumb to economic pressure emanating form remunerative corps like coconut, rubber, banana etc. Due to this change in cropping pattern Kerala has to depend other states for its food requirement mainly for rice. The rice procesisng mills throughout Kerala suffering from shortage of its only rawmaterials-paddy-for processing.

The deceleration in production of rice is due to negative change in the cropping pattern effect in the state of Kerala.Enquiry in to the causes that led to the deceleration of rice production of Kerala during the reference period from 1974-75 to 2003-04 is divided in to three T.E and 1994-95 is the base year. Th period of study were–period -I 1974-75 to 1980-81 , Period -II 1981-82to 1991-92, Period-III 1992-93 to 2003-04 the total output growth decomposed in to three effects using the formula:

Out put growth = $A + S\,W_iC_{it}Y_{it} - A_oSW_iC_{io}\,Y_{io}$

1. Three effects are area effect, yield effect and cropping pattern effect. Out put growth is the sum total of Area effect, yield effect and cropping pattern effect. The decomposition analysis revealed that the tendency of out put growth before and after the bench mark year shows the declining nature of output growth. Value of absolute area effect remains negative before and after the base year shows the stable nature, Yield effect increasing nature and value of cropping pattern effect changes from positive to negative shows the declining of the effect. The tendency of deteriorating the

production of rice every year created raw material shortage to the rice mills through out the state, especially the rice mill cluster in and around Kalady.

2. While analysing the causes and factors led to the clustering of rice mills in and around Kalady and to address the issue in conformity with the Porter's Diamond model of clustering , it is proved that certain locational factors are influencing the clustering of modern rice mills in and around Kalady. From time immemorial Kalady was a trading centre for rice, the demand for 'Kalady rice' still continues. The traditional rice processing families and the younger generation are still continuing as the rice mill owners and traders of rice in this area. The entrepreneurial growth tendencies of this area along with the availability of pure water from the perennial water source of river Periyar are the dominant locational factors that influence the clustering of modern rice mills in and around Kalady. This is proved by applying the proportion test. There is a positive relation between entrepreneurial growth and availability of pure water resulted in the clustering of modern rice mills in and around Kalady.

3. Modern rice mills are classified on the basis of technological progress i.e. highly advanced (fully automated) and advanced (Semi-automated) modern rice mills. The highly advanced rice mills are using sophisticated methods for processing, sorting etc. They are using computer sortex machines. It is proved that technological progress bears a positive influence on sales. The highly advanced modern mills have an upper edge over advanced modern mills over total sales.

4. Technically progressed mills have lesser debt-equity ratio. As already stated that of the 20 modern rice mills selected for financial performances analysis, is divided into two categories i.e (1) Highly Advanced Modern

Rice Mills and (2) Advanced Modern Rice Mills. It is proved that the highly advanced modern rice mills are running in a low gearing-i.e the ratio between proprietors funds and out siders fund are comparitivley low.

5. The most pertinent finding of the study is that the capital and long term funds and properly and fruitfully invested in fixed assets and working capital (Net Current Assets). Apart from this major finding, the other notable findings of the present study are listed below.

OTHER FINDINGS OF THE STUDY

- Kerala is one the state which has the lowest percentage of area of cultivation in India ie.0.76 per cent of the total area of rice cultivation in India.
- Kerala witnessed a decline of 5 lakh ha of land under rice cultivation over a period of two decades.
- Productivity of rice in Kerala shows an upward trend because of the use of HYV seeds.
- During the year 1965-66 about 32.1 per cent of the total land area is under rice cultivation but during the year 2003-04 it reduced 12.01 per cent.
- In Kerala remunerative crops like coconut, rubber, banana etc. increased their proportion of area under cultivation and it resulted in the decrease in the area of rice cultivation.
- Wage rate of agricultural labourers is the highest in Kerala than all other states in India.
- The wage rate agricultural labourers increased about 2500 per cent (25times) when compared to the wage rate of 1970-71.
- The price of paddy per quintal is increased only 3 times when compared to the price of 1970-71.
- The cost of cultivation per quintal is Rs.522 in Kerala which is highest of all other states in India.
- The number of modern rice mills was increased from 6 during 1970 to 35610 in the country during 2004.

- Rice bran is the main by- product of the rice processing industry.
- The growth of Kalady rice mill cluster was rapid after 1980.
- In Kerala 120 modern rice mills are operating and producing about 6 lakh tonnes of processed rice.
- Majority of modern rice mills works on shift basis and the time required for one shift is 8 hours.
- Majority of rice mills (76per cent) met their capital needs through banks and other financial institutions.
- Rice mills are classified into Highly advanced and Advanced rice mills, only 36per cent are highly advanced, others are using advanced moderate technology.only 36 per cent of the units are fully automated and 64 per cent are semi-automated.
- There is not a single unit working in and around Kalady on traditional lines.
- There is not a single unit in and around Kalady owned and operated by government or co-operative sector.
- Majority of rice mills are (67per cent) operated in partnership basis, 19 per cent are soletradership and 14 per cent are private limited companies.
- Majority (79percnt) are working on 50-75per cent capacity utilization.
- Majority (55per cent) of the entrepreneurs have got primary education, 15per cent are graduates, and 3per cent are post graduates: others have either secondary or technical education.(27%).
- Majority (65per cent) are in the age group of 40-50 category 18 per cent are above 50 categories, 17 per cent belong to 30-40 categories.
- 96per cent of the entrepreneurs are locals (in and around Kalady) 4 per cent from within the district of Ernakulam.
- 93 per cent of the rice mill units have their own premises and 4 per cent are operating in rented premises.

- 38per cent of the units employed 25 persons, 24per cent units in between 25-40, only 3 per cent above 40.
- 50per cent of the skilled workers belong to the local area and 50 per cent from outside the local area and out side the state.
- All the skilled and un-skilled workers belong to male category.
- Majority (55per cent) of the skilled workers are from outside the state.
- Majority (88per cent) of the administrative staff are from the local area and 12 per cent from outside the local area and outside the state.
- 68 per cent of the administrative staff are graduated, 22 per cent are post graduates, 2% primary education and 8% have acquired secondary education.
- Majorities (72per cent) of the administrative staff are male category and 28 per cent are females.
- All the units (100 per cent) are producing 'matta variety' of rice.
- In Majority of the units (52 per cent), samples of paddy are verified by the owners of the rice mills.
- 79 per cent of the rice mills purchasing paddy on daily basis, 14 per cent on alternatives days.
- 93 per cent of the units have their own storage facilities others have rented storage facilities.
- Majority of the cases (53 per cent), price of paddy is determined by open/secret negotiation between paddy brokers/commission agents, vendors, and rice mill owners.
- Price of rice is determined by the rice mill owners in consultation with the Government agencies.
- 65per cent of the units reported that they are making sales only in the state of Kerala.
- 32 units have joint–business activities.
- The paddy open market yard at Kalady is the biggest paddy market in Kerala.

- 'LEADS' is the common brand name of the rice bran oil marketed by the Kalady Rice Millers Consortium (KRMC)

SUGGESTIONS AND RECOMMENDATIONS

The following measurers are suggested to remove the problems mentioned earlier to strengthen the development of modern rice mills in and around Kalady:

1. In Kerala production of rice is deteriorating steadily every year. The cluster of modern rice mills in Kalady is to depend on other states for its raw paddy requirement. It is necessary to increase the paddy production by cultivating more paddy fields. The reasons for the deterioration of paddy production is due to increased cost of production, smallsized holdings, lack of irrigation facilities, conversion of paddy fields for construction purposes such as the construction of roads, schools, colleges, houses etc.The main reason is the negative change in cropping pattern i e. more remunerative crops such as coconut, rubber, banana etc are cultivating in the paddy fields .For increasing paddy production the state govern ment should introduce a legislation like the Forest protection. Act that the paddy fields shall not be used for other purposes.
2. The Minimum Support Price of paddy per quintal should increase to meet the cost of production.
3. Declare Kerala as a paddy protection area.
4. Organise a paddy technology mission so that the farmers shall get good prices for the by products also.
5. The Kerala Agricultural University should take necessary R&D activities so that they can introduce HYV seeds to increase the paddy production.
6. Open new agro clinic centers and paddy information centers.
7. Provide infrastructural facilities such as irrigation, electricity, fertilizers etc to the farmers.

8. The Kerala State Electricity Board, a supporting industry of modern rice mill cluster in Kalady should reduce the present power tariff rates as the industry providing staple food to the people of Kerala.
9. Setting up of a common effluent treatment plant for treating effluents generated from the cluster of rice mills in and around Kalady.
10. Setting up of a common fuel pump for the use of modern rice mill cluster members in Kalady. This will considerably reduce the cost of fuel charges.
11. Setting up of a common testing laboratory for the use of modern rice mill cluster members in Kalady.
12. The Food Corporation of India should collect paddy from different parts of the country and the finished product also handover to the FCI so that the rice mill cluster in Kalady can fully utitlise its present capacity in full. This will ultimately reduce the commission / brokerage paid to middlemen in rice trade.
13. A technology-cum-business information centre should be established and it should provide necessary training etc. to its workers, management staff etc.
14. Establish a captive power plant independent bio-gas operated generator sets to reduce the cost of power.
15. A refinery project will help to increase the realisation of product from the expelling plant. The refined oil should be sold in a common brand.
16. Development of new marketing channels in addition to the existing domestic market channels. Women identified through the 'kudumbasree' Programme can be trained and sold the products through this way. This will enable the door-to-door marketing of products of rice mill cluster members.
17. Common marketing yard inside and out side the state should be opened to procure paddy. This will help to procure paddy seasonally so that the modern rice mill cluster can work at full capacity level.

18. Quality control laboratory to test the bran and bran oil is to be established so that the modern rice mills can make use of their by products fully.
19. Linkages with the government agencies such as the industries department, Kerala Agricultural University, Cochin University of Science and Technology (CUSAT), Central food technology research institute (CFTRI) pollution control board, KSEB etc. should be developed.
20. At present only one extraction unit in the ownership of the cluster members is working , steps should be taken to set up more rice bran oil extraction units to extract more rice bran oil and its conversion in to edible oil as well as industrial purpose.
21. For getting jute bags, polythene bags, and other packing materials a consortium owned factory should be established to manufacture packing materials.
22. A fly ash brick manufacturing unit should be established by the cluster members with the help of the government of Kerala to use the fly-ash generated after boiling the plant. This will get value addition for their industrial waste.
23. A common warehouse should be set up by the cluster members to avoid their storage problem.
24. The activities of the 'common store' facilities for storage and supply of mill stores (viz. consumables such as gears, shafts and belt drives) rubber tyres and vehicle spare parts should be popularised and readily available to members of the cluster with out delay.
25. The cluster of modern rice mills should take proper initiative with the co-operation of Kerala Agricultural University and the government agencies to encourage the farmers to shift high yielding and Value yielding varieties of rice. So also the farmers should also provided with all other facilities required for the atmosphere of cultivation in the state. The cluster

along with other specialised institutions as to help the farmers appropriately orient cropping patterns towards paddy and also corporate farming or cluster farming. This will contribute much towards enhancing availability of raw material.

26. The government and the cluster members of modern rice mills should reach an agreement to distribute the products of modern rice mill cluster through the public distribution system(PDS) operated and managed by Kerala Civil Supplies Corporation (Government agency). This will definitely reduce the transportation cost and the danger of bad debt to a greater extend.
27. Various training programmes including 3 month long training Programme to promote export sponsored by SIDBI (State Industries development Bank of India) and implemented by EDI should be launched continuously.
28. The government agencies in this sector should take strict measures for the adherence of quality parameters by the modern rice mill units in respect of each of the brands brought out by them.
29. The government agencies should take necessary steps to control the blending of dyes and chemicals which are injurious to health by some of the rice mills to make the inferior quality rice in attractive forms.
30. Rice mills in Kerala should include in the high priority sector by the government considering its role in supplying the staple food for the 'Keralaites'.
31. A standardised pricing policy after consultation with all those who related to this industry should be formed by the government agencies for the fixation of fair price for the rice processed by the cluster members.
32. The government agencies should encourage the quality control, social services, and environment friendly awards to the best modern rice mills in this sector which satisfies the above parameters.

33. Co-operative paddy procurement scheme should be implemented.
34. Procurement scheme must be given more emphasis and liberal financial assistance from the financial institutions to the co-operative sector to attain the objective is to be made, so that un-holy existence of middlemen can be eliminated effectively.

SUGGESTIONS FOR FURTHER RESEARCH

As stated earlier that the study can be conducted from different angles such as owners, consumers, workers, traders etc. but the present study is limited from the point of view of rice mill owners and workers alone. Further study can be conducted from the point of view of consumers, traders; paddy brokers/ commission agents, paddy farmers, rice traders etc. Another important scope for further research in this area is to examine the problem and prospectus of o value addition and value creation (forward linkages) of by-products such as rice bran, husk etc. Another researchable topic is the various implications of the supporting industries linkages-backward aswellas forward aspects. The rice mill sector give direct employment to 4000 persons .The employer-employee relationship, Labour welfare measures , role of trade unions etc.have further researchable topic. As there is wide gap between demand and supply of rice in Kerala, the possibilities for government owned and operated or co-operative sector can also be studied.